DATA STRUCTURE IN 'C'

DATA STRUCTURE IN 'C'

Edited by

Sudhir Dawra

ANMOL PUBLICATIONS PVT. LTD.

NEW DELHI - 110 002 (INDIA)

ANMOL PUBLICATIONS PVT. LTD.
4374/4B, Ansari Road, Daryaganj
New Delhi - 110 002
Ph.: 23261597, 23278000
Visit us at: www.anmolpublications.com

Data Structure in 'C'

First Edition, 2003

PRINTED IN INDIA

Published by J.L. Kumar for Anmol Publications Pvt. Ltd., New Delhi - 110 002 and Printed at Mehra Offset Press, Delhi.

Contents

Preface

The present volume is a comprehensive set of information about the Data Structure in 'C' language. Various techniques and algorithms are implemented in Programming.

The book is basically focuses on Data Structures and its various procedures for storing and retreiving from the memory. Different methods like Arrays, Stacks, String, Linked List, Recurs, Sort, Tree and Graphs are included in this book.

The objective of this book is to throw light in different techniques of Data Structure in 'C'.

This book is primarily prepared for students pursuing BCA, MCA, B.Tech. and M.Tech. I shall be failing in my duty if I don't acknowledge the contribution of my father Sh. J. K. Dawra and my family support. The last but not least, I am grateful to Anmol Publications Pvt. Ltd. for the undertaking publication of this book.

Any suggestions for the improvement of the book would be welcome and gratefully acknowledged and made use in a subsequent edition.

—Sudhir Dawra

Arrays

Program 1

```
/* Find Inverse of a Matrix */
/* INVERSE.C */

# include<stdio.h>

int i, j;

void display( int, int,  float mat[10][10],float
mat1[10][10]);
void input( int, int,  float mat[10][10],float
mat1[10][10]);
Inverse_Mat(int , int,  float mat[10][10],float
mat1[10][10]);
void swap(int, int, int,  float mat[10][10],float
mat1[10][10]);

/* This function exchange two rows of a matrix */

void swap( int row1,int row2, int col, float
mat[10][10],float mat1[10][10])
{
    for( i = 0; i < col; i++)
    {
        float   temp = mat[row1][i];
        mat[row1][i] = mat[row2][i];
        mat[row2][i] = temp;

        temp = mat1[row1][i];
        mat1[row1][i] = mat1[row2][i];
        mat1[row2][i] = temp;
    }
}
```

(Contd.)

```
/* This function find inverse of matrix */
int Inverse_Mat(int row1, int col1, float
mat[10][10],float mat1[10][10])
{
    int singular = 0;
    int r, c;
    for(r = 0;( r < row1)&& !singular;  r++)
    {

        if( mat[r][r] )  /*  Diagonal element is not
                             zero */
            for(c = 0; c < col1; c++)
                if( c == r)
                {

/* Make all the elements above and below the
current principal diagonal element zero */

    float ratio =  mat[r][r];
        for( i = 0; i < col1; i++)
            {
                mat[r][i] /= ratio ;
                mat1[r][i] /= ratio;
            }
        }
            else
            {
                float ratio = mat[c][r] / mat[r][r];
                    for( i = 0; i < col1;  i++)
                    {
                        mat[c][i]-= ratio*mat[r][i];
                        mat1[c][i]-= ratio*mat1[r][i];
                    }
                }
        else
        {
/* If principal diagonal element is zero */
        singular = 1;
        for(c = (r+1); (c < col1) && singular; ++c)
            if(mat[c][r])
            {
                singular = 0;
```

(Contd.)

```
/* Find non zero elements in the same column */
                swap(r,c,col1, mat, mat1);
                --r;
                }
        }
    }
    return(!singular);
}

/* To print output this is used */

void display( int row, int col, float
mat[10][10],float mat1[10][10])
{
    printf("\n");
    /* Output of inverse Matrix */
    for( i = 0; i < row; i++)
    {
        for( j = 0; j < col; j++)
        {
            printf("  %f", mat1[i][j]);
        }
        printf("\n");
    }
}

/* input function */

void input( int row, int col, float
mat[10][10],float mat1[10][10])
{
    for( i = 0 ; i< row; i++)
    {
        for( j = 0 ;  j<col; j++)
        {
    printf("Input Value for: %d: %d: ", i+1, j+1);
    scanf("%f", &mat[i][j]);
            mat1[i][j] = 0;
        }
        mat1[i][i] = 1;
    }
    printf("\n Entered Matrix is as follows:\n");
```

(Contd.)

```
        for( i = 0; i < row; i++)
        {
            for( j = 0; j < col; j++)
            {
                printf("   %f", mat[i][j]);
            }
            printf("\n");
        }
    }

    /* main function */

    void main()
    {
        int R, C;
        float mat[10][10];
        float mat1[10][10];
        printf("\n Input number of rows:");
        scanf("%d", &R);
        printf(" Input number of cols:");
        scanf("%d", &C);
        input(R,C, mat, mat1);
        Inverse_Mat(R,C, mat,  mat1);
        printf("\n Inverse of above matrix is as
        follows: \n ");
        display(R,C, mat, mat1);
    }
```

Program 2.

```
    /* Find norm of matrix: Norm a matrix is defined as
    squareroot of the sum of the squares of the
    elements of a matrix */

    /* TWO_NOR.C */

    # include<stdio.h>
    # include<math.h>

    # define row 10
```

(Contd.)

```
# define col 10

int i, j;
float summation;

void display( float mat[row][col], int, int);
void input(float mat[row][col] ,int, int);
float norm_mat(float mat[row][col], int, int);

/* Output function */

void display(float mat[row][col] ,int row1, int
col1)
{
    for(i = 0; i < row1; i++)
    {
        for(j = 0; j < col1; j++)
        {
            printf("  %f", mat[i][j]);
        }
            printf("\n"):
    }
}

/* Input function */

void input(float mat[row][col] ,int row1, int col1)
{
    for(i = 0 ; i< row1; i++)
    {
        for(j = 0 ;  j<col1; j++)
        {
printf("\nInput Value for : %d: %d: ", i+1, j+1);
scanf("%f", &mat[i][j]);
        }
    }
}

/* Calculating norm of a matrix */

float norm_mat( float mat[row][col], int row1, int
col1)
{
```

(Contd.)

```
    summation = 0;
    for(i = 0; i < row1; i++)
    {
       for(j = 0; j < col1; j++)
       {
          summation += mat[i][j] * mat[i][j];
       }
    }
    return(summation);
}

/* main function */

void main()
{
    float mat[row][col];
    int r,c;
    printf("\n Input number of rows:");
    scanf("%d", &r);
    printf("\n Input number of cols:");
    scanf("%d", &c);
    input(mat, r, c);
    printf("\n Entered Two Dimensional array is as
          follows:\n");
    display(mat, r, c);
    printf("\n Norm of above matix is : %f",
          sqrt(norm_mat(mat, r, c)));
}
```

Program 3.

```
/* Subtraction of two Matrices */
/* TWO_SUB.C */

# include<stdio.h>
# include<stdlib.h>

# define row 10
# define col 10

int i, j;
int row1, col1;
int row2, col2;
```

(Contd.)

```
float mat1[row][col];
float mat2[row][col];
float mat_res[row][col];

void mat_sub(  float mat1[row][col], int, int,
float mat2[row][col], int, int,
float mat_res[row][col]);

void display(float mat[row][col], int, int);
void input(float mat[row][col], int , int);

/*  Function mat_sub */

void mat_sub(float mat1[row][col], int row1, int
col1,
float mat2[row][col], int row2, int col2,
float mat_res[row][col])
{
    if(( row1 == row2) && (col1 == col2))
    {
printf("\n Subtraction is possible and Result is as
        follows\n");

        for(i = 0; i < row1; i++)
        for(j = 0; j < col1; j++)
            mat_res[i][j] = mat1[i][j] - mat2[i][j];
            display(mat_res,row1,col1);
    }
    else
        printf("\n Subtraction is not possible");
    exit(0);
}

/* Output Function */

void display(float mat[row][col], int r, int c )
{
    for(i = 0; i < r; i++)
    {
        for(j = 0; j < c; j++)
        {
            printf("  %f", mat[i][j]);
```

(Contd.)

```
        }
            printf("\n");
    }
}

/* Input function */

void input(float mat[row][col], int r, int c)
{
    for(i = 0 ; i< r; i++)
    {
        for(j = 0 ;  j<c; j++)
        {
    printf("Input Value for : %d: %d: ", i+1, j+1);
    scanf("%f", &mat[i][j]);
        }
    }
}

/* main function */

void main()
{
int row1, col1;
int row2, col2;
float mat1[row][col];
float mat2[row][col];
float mat_res[row][col];
printf("\n Input the row  of the matrix->1:");
scanf("%d", &row1);
printf("\n Input the col  of the matrix->1:");
scanf("%d", &col1);
printf(" Input data for matrix-> 1\n");

input(mat1, row1, col1);
printf("Input the row  of the matrix ->2:");
scanf("%d", &row2);
printf(" Input the col  of the matrix->2:");
scanf("%d", &col2);
printf(" Input data for matrix-> 2\n");

input(mat2, row2, col2);
```

(Contd.)

```
printf("\n Entered Matrix First is as follows:\n");
display(mat1,row1,col1);
printf("\n Entered Matrix Two is as follows:\n");
display(mat2,row2,col2);
mat_sub(mat1,row1,col1,mat2,row1,col2,mat_res);
display(mat_res,row2,col2);
}
```

Stack

Program 1.

```
/* PEEP OPERATION ON THE STACK USING ARRAYS */
/* PEEPCH.C */

# include<stdio.h>
# include<string.h>
# include<ctype.h>

# define size  100

int top = -1;
int flag = 0;

int stack[100];
int data;

void push(int *, int);
int peep(int *);
void display(int *);

/* Definition of the push function */

void  push(int s[], int d)
{
    if(top ==(size-1))
            flag = 0;
    else
    {
            flag = 1;
            ++top;
            s[top] = d;
```

(Contd.)

```
    }
}

/* Definition of the peep function */

int peep(int s[])
{
    int i;
    int peeped_element;
    printf("\n Input the information number to which
            you want access:");
    scanf("%d", &i);

    if(top - i + 1 < 0)
    {
            peeped_element = 0;
            flag = 0;
    }
    else
    {
            flag = 1;
            peeped_element = s[top-i +1];
    }
    return (peeped_element);
}

/* Definition of the display function */
void display(int s[])
{
    int i;
    if(top == -1)
    {
            printf("Stack is empty");
    }
    else
    {
            for(i = top; i>=0; --i)
                printf(" %d  ", s[i]);
    }
}

/* Function main */
```

(Contd.)

```
void main()
{
    int  data;
    char choice;
    int q = 0;
    int top = -1;

    do
    {
            printf(" \nPush->i Peep->p Quit->q:");
            printf("\nInput the choice : ");
            do
            {
                    choice = getchar();
                    choice =tolower(choice);
            }
            while(strchr("ipq",choice)==NULL);
            printf("Your choice is: ", choice);
            switch(choice)
            {
            case 'i' :
            printf("\n Input the element to push:");
            scanf("%d", &data);
                    push(stack, data);
                    if(flag)
                    {
                    printf("\n After inserting ");
                            display(stack);
                            if(top == (size-1))
                    printf("\n Stack is full");
                    }
                    else
                    printf("\n Stack overflow after
                    pushing");
                    break;

            case 'p' :
                    data = peep(stack);
                    if(flag)
                    {
            printf("\n Data is peeped: %d", data);
            printf("\n Stack is as follows:\n");
```

(Contd.)

```
                    display(stack);
                }
                else
                printf("\n Stack underflow");
                break;
            case 'q':
                q = 1;
            }
    } while(!q);
}
```

Program 2.

```
/* polish.c */

  # include<malloc.h>
  # include<string.h>
  # include<stdlib.h>

  # define size 5

   void puch(char *, char , int *);
        char pop( char *, int *);
        int letter_match(char );
        void push(char *, int *, char );
        int match_number(char );
        int match_operator(char );
        int operator_precedence(char );
        void polish_fun(char *, char *, int *);
        void error(int, int );

/* Push function */

   void push( char s[], int *s_pointer, char ch)
     {
      if(*s_pointer == size)
        {
        printf("\n Stack overflow");
        }
        else
        {
```

(Contd.)

```
            s[++(*s_pointer)] = ch ;
           }
     }

/* Pop function */

  char pop( char s[], int *s_pointer)
       {
     if(*s_pointer < 0)
      {
      printf("\n Stack underflow");
       return 0;
      }
      else
      {
      return(s[(*s_pointer) -- ]);
      }
       }

/* Definition of function */

  int letter_match(char ch)
       {
         return(((ch>='A')&&(ch<='Z')) ||
((ch>='a')&&(ch <= 'z')));
       }

/* Definition of the function */

 int  match_number( char ch)
      {
        return((ch >='0') && (ch<='9'));
      }

/* Definition of the function */

  int match_operator(char ch)
      {
      int i;
        char operator[6];

             operator[0] = '+';
```

(Contd.)

```
            operator[1] = '-';
            operator[2] = '*';
            operator[3] = '/';
            operator[4] = '%';

        for(i = 0; i < 5; i ++)
            {
              if(ch == operator[i])
                return(1);
              else
                return(0);
            }
        }

/* Definition of the function */

  int operator_precedence(char ch)
      {
        int preced;
        switch(ch)
       {
         case '(' : preced = 0; break;
         case '+' :
         case '-' : preced = 1; break;
         case '*' :
         case '/' : preced = 2; break;
         case '%' : preced = 3; break;
       }
      return(preced);
      }

/* Definition of the function */

   void polish_fun(char infix[], char suffix[], int
    *err)
       {
      char ch, last =')';
      char stack[size];
      int i = 0;
      int s_pointer = -1;
      int bracket = 1;
      int ifp,sfp = 0;
```

(Contd.)

```
      push(stack, &s_pointer,'(');
        do
          {
           while(infix[i] ==' ')
           ++i;
           ifp = i;
           ch = infix[ifp];
    switch(ch)
    {
    case '(':
if(letter_match(last)||match_number(last) || (last
== ')'))
          {
            *err = 1;
            error(1,ifp+1);
          }
          ++bracket ;
         push(stack,&s_pointer,ch);
          break;
     case '+':
     case '-':
     case '*':
     case '/':
     case '%':

      if(match_operator(last)||(!letter_match(last)&&
!match_number(last)&&(last!=')')))
      {
        *err = 1;
        error(2,ifp+1);
      }

      while(operator_precedence(stack[s_pointer]
>=operator_precedence(ch))
        suffix[sfp++]=pop(stack,&s_pointer);
        push(stack,&s_pointer,ch);
        break;

     case ')':
       if(match_operator(last)
     { *err = 1;
        error(2,ifp+1);
```

(Contd.)

```
 }

 if(last == '(')
    {
        *err = 1;
        error(2,ifp+1);
        error(1,ifp+1);
    }

 while(stack[s_pointer] != '(' && s_pointer > 0)
   suffix[sfp++] = pop(stack, &s_pointer);
   --s_pointer;
   --bracket;
   break;

   case  ' ': while(infix[ifp+1] == ' ' &&
infix[ifp])
        ++ifp;
        break;
  default:
        if(letter_match(last)||math_number(last))
          {
            *err = 1;
            error(1,ifp+1);
            error(5,ifp+1);
          }

          if (letter_match(ch))
            suffix[sfp++] = infix[ifp];
            else
             if (match_number(ch))
               {
                while(match_number(infix[ifp]))
                   suffix[sfp++] = infix[ifp++];
                   --ifp;
                }

                else error(4,ifp+1);
             } /* end of switch */

 last = infix[ifp];
 ++ifp;
```

(Contd.)

```
i = ifp;
} while(infix[ifp]);

suffix[sfp] = 0;
if(bracket)
  {
    *err =1;
    error(3,ifp-1);
  }
}
break;
```

```
/* Definition of the function */

void input(char infix[])
  {
    int i = 0;
    printf("\nInput the infix expression: ");
    gets(infix);
    i = strlen(infix);
    printf("\n Entered expression is :");
    gets(infix);
    infix[i] = ')';
    infix[i+1] = '\0';
  }
```

```
/* Definition of the function */

void error(int n, int ifp)
  {
    switch(n)
    {
  case 1: printf("\n Error->1:Missing operator");
  case 2: printf("\n Error->2:Missing operand");
  case 3: printf("\n Error->3:Mismatched
          parentheses");
  case 4: printf("\n Error->4:Illegal character
          is expression");
  case 5: printf("\n Error->5:Multicharacter
          variable");
    }
  printf("\n Position of the cursor: %d", ifp);
```

(Contd.)

```
    }

/* Definition of the function main */

    void main()
      {
        int err, ans;
        char infix[size],suffix[size];
        err = 0;
        input(infix);
        polish_fun(infix,suffix, &err);
        if(!err)
          {
          printf("\n The suffix form of the given,
                expression is: ");
           puts(suffix);
          }
      }
```

Program 3.

```
/* postfix.c */

# include<stdio.h>
# include<string.h>
# include<ctype.h>
# include<stdlib.h>

# define Arnold '\0'
# define Blank ' '
# define Tab '\t'

#define Maxlen 64
static char infix [Maxlen+1], stack[Maxlen],
postfix[Maxlen+1];

# define Empty (-1) /* empty stack */
static int top;

/* symbol types */

#define Operator (-10)
```

(Contd.)

```
# define Operand (-20)

# define LeftParen (-30)
# define RightParen (-40)

static char *symbols = "()+-%*/";

/* Symbol precedence */

# define LeftParenPrec 0  /* ( */
# define AddPrec 1 /* + */
# define SubPrec 1 /* - */
# define MultPrec 2 /* * */
# define DivPrec 2 /* / */
# define RemPrec 2 /* % */
# define None 999 /* all else */

void read_input(void);
void infix_to_postfix(void);
void write_output(void);
void push(char symbol);
char pop (void);

int get_type(char );
int get_prec(char );
int white_space(char );

void full_stack();
void empty_stack();

void main()
{
    char ans[2];
    do
    {
            top = Empty; /* reset stack */
            read_input();
            infix_to_postfix();
            write_output();

            /* Selection */

            printf("\n\n Another (y/n)");
```

(Contd.)

```
        gets(ans);
    } while (toupper(ans[0]) == 'Y');
}

/* function infix to postfix conversion */
void infix_to_postfix(void)
{
    int i,p, len, type, precedence;
    char next ;

    /* i for infix, p for postfix */

    i = p = 0;
    len = strlen(infix);

    /* loop through input string */
    while(i < len)
    {
    /* ignore whitepsce in infix expression */
            if( !white_space(infix[i]))
            {
                    type = get_type(infix[i]);
                    switch(type)
                    {
            /* push left paren onto stack */
                    case LeftParen:
                            push(infix[i]);
                            break;

            /* pop stack until matching left paren */
                    case RightParen:
                    while((next = pop()) != '(')
                            postfix[p++] = next;
                            break;
            case Operand: postfix[p++] = infix[i];
                            break;
 /* Pop stack until first operator of higher
 precedence and then stack this operator */
                    case Operator:
                            precedence =
 get_prec(infix[i]);
```

(Contd.)

```
    /* Anything on stack to pop */
            while(top > Empty && precedence<=
get_prec(stack[top]))
                            postfix[p++] = pop();
                            push(infix[i]);
                            break;
                    }
            }
    i++; /* next symbol in infix expression */
    }

    /* pop any remaining operators */
    while(top > Empty )
            postfix[p++] = pop();
    postfix[p] = Arnold ; /* ensure a string */
}

/* Function to find operator type */

int get_type(char symbol )
{
    switch(symbol)
    {
    case '(' :
            return (LeftParen);
    case ')':
            return (RightParen);
    case '+':
    case '-':
    case '%':
    case '*':
    case '/':
            return (Operator);
    default:
            return (Operand);
    }
}

/* Find precedence of the operator */

int get_prec(char symbol )
{
```

(Contd.)

```
    switch(symbol)
    {
    case '+':
            return (AddPrec);
    case '-':
            return (SubPrec);
    case '*':
            return (MultPrec);
    case '/':
            return (DivPrec);
    case '%':
            return (RemPrec);
    case '(':
            return (LeftParenPrec);
    default:
            return (None);
    }
}

/* Function push */

void push(char symbol)
{
    /* check for overflow */
    if(top > Maxlen)
            full_stack();
    else
            stack[++top] = symbol;
}

/* Function pop */

char pop(void)
{
    /* check for underflow */
    if (top <= Empty )
            empty_stack();
    else
            return (stack[top--]);
}

/* Exit in case of overflow */
```

(Contd.)

```
void full_stack(void )
{
    printf("\n Full Stsck ... exiting. \n");
    exit(1);
}

/* Exit in case of underflow */

void empty_stack(void)
{
    printf("\n Empty Stack ... exiting \n");
    exit(2);
}

void read_input(void)
{
    printf("\n Infix (up to %d chars): ", Maxlen);
    gets(infix);
}


/* Output function */
void write_output(void)
{
    printf("\n Infix: %s", infix);
    printf("\n Postfix: %s \n",postfix);
}

/* function white space checking */

int white_space(char symbol)
{
    return( symbol == Blank || symbol == Tab ||
symbol == Arnold);
}
```

Program 4.

```
/* INSERTION AND DELETION IN A QUEUE ARRAY
IMPLEMENTATION */

/* queue_a.c */
```

(Contd.)

```
# include<stdio.h>
# include<string.h>
# include<ctype.h>
# include<stdlib.h>

# define size 10
int rear, front;
int ch;
int q[size];

int rear = 0;
int front = 0;
void Insert_queue();
void Delete_queue();
void Display_queue();

/* Function to create queue */

void  Insert_queue()
{
   printf("\n Input the element :");
   scanf("%d", &ch);
   if(rear < size)
   {
         rear ++;
         q[rear] = ch ;
         if(front == 0)
               front = 1;
   }
   else
         printf("\n Queue is overflow");
}

/* Function to perform delete operation */

void Delete_queue()
{
   if (front == 0)
   {
         printf("\n Underflow");
         return ;
   }
```

(Contd.)

```
        else
        {
                ch = q[front];
                printf("\n Element deleted : %d", ch);
        }
        if(front == rear)
        {
                front = 0;
                rear = 0;
        }
        else
                front = front + 1;
}

/* Output function */

void Display_queue()  //char q[])
{
        int i;
        if (front == 0)
                return;
        for(i = front ; i <= rear; i++)
                printf(" %d ", q[i]);
}

/* Function main */

void main()
{
        int k = 0;
        char choice;

        do
        {
                printf("\nInsert->i Delete->d Quit->q:");
                printf("\nInput the choice : ");
                do
                {
                        choice = getchar();
                        choice = tolower(choice);
                }while(strchr("idq",choice)==NULL);
                printf("Your choice is: %c ", choice);
```

(Contd.)

```
            switch(choice)
            {
    case 'i' :
            Insert_queue();
            printf("\nQueue after inserting ");
                    Display_queue();
                    break;

    case 'd' :
            Delete_queue();
            printf("\nQueue content after deleteion
                     is as follows:\n");
                    Display_queue();
                    break;

    case 'q':
            k = 1;
            }
    } while(!k);
}
```

Program 5.

```
/* INSERTION AND DELETION IN A CIRCULAR QUEUE ARRAY
IMPLEMENTATION */

/* QUEUEID.C */

# include<stdio.h>
# include<string.h>
# include<ctype.h>
# include<stdlib.h>

# define size 6

int L, U;  /* L means lower bound U means upper
              bound */

int rear, front;
int ch;
int q[size];
```

(Contd.)

```
int rear = -1;
int front = -1;
void Insert_queue();
void Delete_queue();
void Display_queue();

/* Function to create queue */

void Insert_queue()
{
            if ((front == 0) && (rear == size-1))
            {
                    printf("\n Overflow");
                    rear = 1;
                    return;
            }
            else
            if (front < 0) /* Insert first element */
            {
                    front = 0;
                    rear = 0;
                    printf("\nInput the element :");
                    scanf("%d", &ch);
                    q[rear] = ch ;
            }
            else
                    if (rear == size-1)
            {
                    rear = 0;
                    printf("\n Input the element :");
                    scanf("%d", &ch);
                    q[rear] = ch ;
            }
            else
            {
                    rear ++;
                    printf("\n Input the element :");
                    scanf("%d", &ch);
                    q[rear] = ch ;
                    }
}
```

(Contd.)

```
/* Function to perform delete operation */

void Delete_queue()
{
    if (front < 0)
    {
        printf("\nUnderflow");
        return ;
    }
        ch = q[front];
        q[front] = NULL;
        printf("\n Element deleted :", ch);
    if(front == rear)
    {
        front = -1;
        rear = -1;
    }
    else
    if ( front == size-1)
    {
        front = 0;
    }
    else
    {
        front++ ;
    }

}

/* Output function */

void Display_queue()
{
    int i;
    if (front < 0)
        return;
    if ( rear >= front)
    {
        for(i = front; i <= rear; i++)
        {
            printf("\n i = %d", i);
            printf(" %d ", q[i]);
```

(Contd.)

```
            }
        }
        else
        {
            for(i = front; i < size; i++)
            {
                printf("\n i = %d", i);
                printf(" %d", q[i]);
            }
            for(i = 0; i <= rear; i++)
            {
                printf("\n i = %d", i);
                printf(" %d ", q[i]);
            }
        }
    }

    /* Function main  */
    void main()
    {
        int k = 0;
        char choice;

        do
        {
            printf("\nInsert->i Delete->d Quit->q:");
            printf("\nInput the choice : ");
            do
            {
                choice = getchar();
                choice = tolower(choice);
            }while(strchr("idq",choice)==NULL);
            printf("Your choice is: %c",choice);

            switch(choice)
            {
        case 'i' :
            Insert_queue();
            printf("\nQueue after inserting ");
            Display_queue();
            break;
```

(Contd.)

```
      case 'd' :
             Delete_queue();
             printf("\nQueue content after deleteion
                     is as follows:\n");
             Display_queue();
             break;
      case 'q':
             k = 1;
             }
      } while(!k);
}
```

Program 6.

```
/* IMPLEMENTATION OF THE STACK USING ARRAYS */
/* STACK_A.C */

# include<stdio.h>
# include<string.h>
# include<ctype.h>

# define size  100


int top = -1;
int flag = 0;
int stack[size];

void push(int *, int);
int pop(int *);
void display(int *);

/* Definition of the push function */

void push(int s[], int d)
{
    if(top ==(size-1))
           flag = 0;
    else
    {
           flag = 1;
           ++top;
```

(Contd.)

```
            s[top] = d;
      }
}

/* Definition of the pop function */

int pop(int s[])
{
      int popped_element;
      if(top == -1)
      {
            popped_element = 0;
            flag = 0;
      }
      else
      {
            flag = 1;
            popped_element = s[top];
            --top;
      }
      return (popped_element);
}

/* Definition of the display function */

void display(int s[])
{
      int i;
      if(top == -1)
      {
            printf("\n Stack is empty");
      }
      else
      {
            for(i = top; i >= 0; --i)
                  printf("\n %d", s[i] );
      }
}

/* Function main */

void main()
```

(Contd.)

```
{
    •
    int  data;
    char choice;
    int q = 0;
    int top = -1;

    do
    {
        printf(" \nPush->i Pop->p Quit->q:");
        printf("\nInput the choice : ");
          do
          {
                choice = getchar();
                choice =tolower(choice);
          }while(strchr("ipq",choice)==NULL);
        printf("Your choice is: %c",choice);

          switch(choice)
          {
    case 'i' :
        printf("\n Input the element to push:");
        scanf("%d", &data);
                push(stack, data);
                if(flag)
                {
        printf("\n After inserting ");
                      display(stack);
                      if(top == (size-1))
        printf("\n Stack is full");
                }
                else
        printf("\n Stack overflow after pushing");
                break;

    case 'p' :
                data = pop(stack);
                if(flag)
                {
        printf("\n Data is popped: %d", data);
        printf("\n Rest data in stack is as
                follows:\n");
```

(Contd.)

```
                    display(stack);
                }
                else
                printf("\n Stack underflow" );
                break;
            case 'q':
                q = 1;
            }
    } while(!q);
}
```

Program 7.

```
/* STACK IMPLEMENTATION USING LINKED LIST */
/* STACK_L.C */

# include<stdio.h>
# include<malloc.h>

struct link
{
    int info;
    struct link *next;
} *start;


void display(struct link *);
struct link *push(struct link *);
struct link *pop(struct link *);
int main_menu();

void display(struct link *rec)
{
    while(rec != NULL)
    {
            printf(" %d ",rec->info);
            rec = rec->next;
    }
}

struct link * push(struct link *rec)
{
```

(Contd.)

```
    struct link *new_rec;
    printf("\n Input the new value for next location
            of the stack:");

    new_rec = (struct link *)malloc(sizeof(struct
                link));
    scanf("%d", &new_rec->info);
    new_rec->next = rec;
    rec = new_rec;
    return(rec);
}
struct  link * pop(struct link *rec)
{
    struct link *temp;

    if(rec == NULL)
    {
          printf("\n Stack is empty");
    }
    else
    {
    temp = rec->next;
    free(rec);
    rec = temp;
    printf("\n After pop operation the stack is as
            follows:\n");
    display(rec);
    if(rec  == NULL)
    printf("\n Stack is empty");
    }
    return(rec);
}

int main_menu ()
{
    int choice;
    do
    {
    printf("\n 1<-Push ");
    printf("\n 2<-Pop");
    printf("\n 3<-Quit");
    printf("\n Input your choice :");
```

(Contd.)

```
    scanf("%d", &choice);
    if(choice <1 || choice >3)
    printf("\n Incorrect choice-> Try once again");
    } while(choice <1 || choice >3);

    return(choice);
}


/* main function */

void main()
{
    struct link *start ;
    int choice;
    start = NULL;
    do
    {
            choice = main_menu();
            switch(choice)
            {
    case 1:
            start = push(start);
            printf("\n After push operation stack is
                    as follows:\n");
            display(start);
            break;
    case 2:
            start = pop(start);
            break;
            default :
            printf("\n End of session");
            }
    } while(choice != 3);
}
```

Program 8.

```
/* UPDATING A STACK IMPLEMENTED WITH THE HELP OF
ARRAYS.*/
/* UPDATE.C */
# include<stdio.h>
```

(Contd.)

```
# include<string.h>
# include<ctype.h>
# define size  100

int top = -1;
int flag = 0;

int stack[100];
int data;
void push (int *, int);
int update (int *);
void display (int *);

/* Definition of the push function */

void push(int s[], int d)
{
    if(top ==(size-1))
            flag = 0;
    else
    {
            flag = 1;
            ++top;
            s[top] = d;
    }
}

/* Definition of the pop function */

int update(int s[])
{
    int i;
    int update_element;
    printf("\n Input the information number to which
            you want to update: ");
    scanf("%d", &i);

    if(top - i + 1 < 0)
    {
            update_element = 0;
            flag = 0;
    }
```

(Contd.)

```
    else
    {
            flag = 1;
            update_element = s[top-i +1];
            printf("\n Input the new value: ");
            scanf("%d", &s[top-i+1]);
    }
    return (update_element);
}

/* Definition of the display function */

void display(int s[])
{
    int i;
    if(top == -1)
    {
            printf("Stack is empty");
    }
    else
    {
            for(i = top; i>=0; --i)
                    printf(" %d", s[i]);
    }
}

void main()
{
    int stack[size];
    int  data;
    char choice;
    int q = 0;
    int top = -1;

    do
    {
            printf(" \nPush->i Update->u Quit->q: ");
            printf("\nInput the choice : ");
            do
            {
                    fflush(stdin);
                    choice = getchar();
```

(Contd.)

```
            choice = tolower(choice);
        }while(strchr("iuq",choice)==NULL);
        printf("Your choice is -> %c", choice);

        switch(choice)
        {
    case 'i' :
    printf("\n Input the element to pushed: ");
    scanf("%d", &data);
    push(stack, data);
    if(flag)
        {
        printf("\n After inserting ");
        display(stack);
        if(top == (size-1))
        printf("\n Stack is full");
        }
    else
    printf("\n Stack overflow after pushing");
    break;

    case 'u' :
    data = update(stack);
    if(flag)
        {
        printf("\n Data is peepped: %d", data);
        printf("\n Stack is as follows:\n");
        display(stack);
        }
    else
        printf("\n Stack underflow");
        break;
    case 'q':
        q = 1;
        }
    } while(!q);
}
```

String

Program 1.

```
/* Delete a substring from a string */
/* DELET.C */

# include<stdio.h>
# include<string.h>

int index_str1,index_str2,k;
int c[100];

int str_del_loc(char *, char *, int *);

/* Function str_del_loc that finds location of the
sub-string and delete. */

int  str_del_loc(char *s1, char *s2, int c[])
{
   int j, count = 0;
   int i, l =0;
   for(index_str1 = 0;  s1[index_str1];
index_str1++)
      for(index_str2=index_str1, k = 0;
s1[index_str2] == s2[k]&&s1[index_str1];
index_str2++, k++)
         if( !s2[k+1])
         {
            count ++;
            c[l++] = index_str1;
            for(j = index_str1, i =
strlen(s2)+index_str1; s1[i]; j++, i++)
               s1[j] = s1[i];
            s1[j] = NULL;
```

(Contd.)

```
        printf("\n After delete operation the
                output %s", s1);
        }
    return(count);
}

/* Function main */

void main()
{
    char *s;
    int c[100];
    char s1[]="Ram Bahadur Bahadur Patel";
    char s2[] ="Baha";
    int count;
    count = str_del_loc (s1, s2,c);
    printf("\n Number of occurences = %d", count);
}
```

Program 2.

```
/* Find locations of a substring in a string */
/* LO_NO.C */

# include<stdio.h>
# include<string.h>

int index_str1,index_str2,k;
int c[100];

int str(char *, char *, int *);
int Number_occ(char *, char *, int *);

/* Function str that finds locations of the sub-
string */

int str(char *s1, char *s2, int c[])
{
    int count = 0;
    int l =0;
    for(index_str1 = 0;  s1[index_str1];
index_str1++)
```

(Contd.)

```
        for(index_str2=index_str1, k = 0;
s1[index_str2] == s2[k]&&s1[index_str1];
index_str2++, k++)
             if(!s2[k+1])
             {
                count ++;
                c[l++] = index_str1;
             }

     return(count);
}

/* Function main */

void main()
{
     char *s;
     int c[100];
     int location ;
     char s1[]="Ram Bahadur Bahadur Patel";
     char s2[] ="Baha";
     int i, loc;
     int count;

     count = str (s1, s2,c);

     printf("\n Number of occurences = %d", count);

     for(i = 0;i < count; i++)

        {
location = c[i];
s = &s2[0];
printf("\n Starting location = %d|", location+1);
while(*(s++))
        {
           putchar(s1[location++]);
        }
     }
}
```

Program 3.

```
/* Find location of a substring first start in a
string */
/*  LOCAT.C */

# include<stdio.h>

int index_str1,index_str2,k;
int str(char *, char *);

/* Function str that finds first location of the
sub-string */

int str(char *s1, char *s2)
{
   for(index_str1 = 0;  s1[index_str1];
index_str1++)
      for(index_str2=index_str1, k =0;
s1[index_str2] == s2[k]; index_str2++, k++)
         if( !s2[k+1])
         {
            return(index_str1);
         }
   return(NULL);
}

/*  Function main */

void main()
{
   char *s;
   char s1[]="Ram Bahadur Patel";
   char s2[] ="Baha";
   int location = str (s1, s2);
   s = s2;
   printf("\n Location = %d", location);
   while(*(s++))
   {
      putchar(s1[location++]);
   }
}
```

Program 4.

```
/* Replace a sub-string in a string·*/
/* REPLACE.C*/

# include<stdio.h>
# include<string.h>

int index_str1,index_str2,k;
int c[100];

int str_rep(char *, char *, int *);

/* Function str that finds first location of the
sub-string */

int str_rep(char *s1, char *s2, int c[])
{
   int count = 0;
   int l =0;
   int j, i = 0;
   char s3[]= "Jaunpur";
   for(index_str1 = 0;  s1[index_str1];
index_str1++)
      for(index_str2=index_str1, k = 0;
s1[index_str2] == s2[k]&&s1[index_str1];
index_str2++, k++)
         if(!s2[k+1])
         {
            count ++;
            c[l++] = index_str1;
            for(j = index_str1; j <
strlen(s3)+index_str1;  j++)
               s1[j] = s3[i++];
            printf("\n %s ", s1);
         }

   return(count);
}

/* Function main */
```

(Contd.)

```
void main()
{
    char *s;
    int c[100];
    char s1[]="Ram Bahadur Bahadur Patel";
    char s2[] ="Bahadur";
    int count;
    str_rep(s1, s2,c);
}
```

Program 5.

```
/* strcat.c */

# include<stdio.h>

char *strcat1(char *target, const char *source)
{
    char *original = target;
    while(*target)
          target++;
    while (*target++= *source++);
    return(original);
}

main()
{
    char Name[256]="Ram Bahadur ";
    char Title[256]="Patel";
    strcat1(Name, Title);
    puts(Name);
}
```

Program 6.

```
/* STRING1.C**/

# include<stdio.h>

void main()
{
    char null_string[] = "\0";
```

(Contd.)

```
    char blank_string[] = " ";
    char string[] = "The C is a powerful language";
    printf("\n %s", null_string);
    printf("\n %s", blank_string);
    printf("\n %s", string);
}
```

Program 7.

```
/**  STRING10.C **/

# include<stdio.h>
# include<string.h>
# include<malloc.h>
# include<ctype.h>

void insertion ( char *, int , char *, char *);

/* Function insert */

void insertion ( char *text , int position, char
*s, char *p)
{
    char ch ;
    while(position)
    {
            *p++ = *text++ ;
            position--;
    }
    while(*s)
    {
            *p++ = *s++ ;
    }
    printf("\n After insertion of the pattern\n ");
    printf("there needs blank at right side of the
            pattern(y): ");
    ch  = getchar() ;
    ch = toupper(ch);

    if (ch == 'Y')
            *p++ = ' ';
    while(*text)
```

(Contd.)

```
    {
          *p++ = *text++ ;
    }
    *p = '\0';
}

/* FUnction main */

void main()
{
    char *point ;
    char text[128]="COMPUTER SCIENCE ENGINEERING";
    char s[4] ="AND";
    int position = 17;
    point =(char*) malloc(128);
    printf("\n*********************************\n");
    printf(" TEXT AND PATTERN ARE AS FOLLOWS\n");
    printf("\n*********************************\n");
    printf("\n %s", text);
    printf("\n%s", s);
    printf("\n*********************************\n");
    insertion ( text, position, s, point);
    printf("\n*********************************\n");
    printf("\n %s", point);
    printf("\n*********************************\n");
    printf("\n Press a key");
    getchar();
}
```

Program 8.

```
/** STRING11.C **/

# include<stdio.h>
# include<string.h>
# include<malloc.h>

void deletion ( char *, int , int , char * );

/* Function delete */

void deletion (char *text, int position, int
```

(Contd.)

```
length, char *p)
{
    while(position)
    {
       *p++ = *text++ ; /* copying the pattern */
       position--;
    }

    while(length)
    {
       *text++; /* skipping the pattern */
       length --;
    }

    *p++ = ' ';
    while(*text)
    {
    *p++ = *text++ ; /* copying the rest of text */
    }
    *p = '\0';
}

/* Function main */

void main()
{
    char *point ;
    char text[128]="COMPUTER SCIENCE AND
ENGINEERING";
    int length = 3 ;
    int position = 17 ;

    point = (char *) malloc(128);

    printf("\n      TEXT IS AS FOLLOWS               ");
    printf("\n**********************************\n");
    printf("\n %s", text);
    printf("\n**********************************\n");
    deletion (text, position, length , point);
    printf("\n OUTPUT AFTER DELETION OF PATTERN ");
    printf("\n**********************************\n");
    printf("\n %s", point);
    printf("\n**********************************\n");
```

(Contd.)

```
    printf("\n Press a key");
    getchar();
}
```

Program 9.

```
/**  STRING12.C **/

# include<stdio.h>
# include<string.h>
# include<malloc.h>
# include<stdlib.h>

/**          Global parameters                          **/

char *buffer;
char pattern1[9];
char pattern2[9];

char *s;
char s1[8];
int size ;
int i, j;
int length;
int l ;
int position ;
int back1, back2 ;

void replacement(char *, char *, char * );

void replacement(char *buffer, char *pattern1, char
*pattern2 )
{
    length = strlen(pattern1);
    s = ( char *) malloc(length);
    printf("Length => %d", length);
    back1 = length ;
    back2 = size ;
    getchar();

    i = 0 ;
    j = 0 ;
```

(Contd.)

```
    l = 0 ;
    position = 0 ;

    while(size)
    {
            size --;
            while(length)
            {
                    position ++ ;
                    if ( buffer[i] == pattern1[j])
                    {
                    if ((position >= back2) ||
(position < 0))
                                    exit(0);
                            s[j] = buffer[i];
                            l ++ ;
                            i ++ ;
                            size --;
                            j ++ ;
                            length --;
                            if( l == back1)
                            {
                                    s[j] = '\0';
printf("\nPATTERN IS FOUND");
printf("\n***************\n");
printf(" LENGTH OF PATTERN: %d ",l);
printf("\n PATTERN IS: %s", s);
printf("\n Starting Position = %d", (position-l));
printf("\n Press a key");
                                    getchar();
                                    l= 0 ;
                                    j = 0 ;
printf("\nPATTERN REPLACEMENT IN PROGRESS");
printf("\n*******************************\n");

    for(i = (position - strlen(pattern2));
        i < position ; i++)
                                    {
    buffer[i] = pattern2[j];

putchar(buffer[i]);
```

(Contd.)

```
                            j++;
                            getchar();
                        }

printf("\n SEE AFTER FIRST PATTERN REPLACEMENT ");
printf("\n ********************************** \n");
printf("\n %s", buffer);
printf("\n Press a key");
                        getchar();

                    } /* end of if */
                } /* end of if */

                else
                {
                    i++;
                    j = 0;
                    l = 0;
                    size -- ;
                    length = back1;
                }

            } /* end first while */
            length = back1 ;
    }     /* end of second while */
}

void main()
{
    FILE *fp ;
    fp = fopen("TEST","r");
    if( fp == NULL )
    {
            printf(" FILE \n");
            perror("ERROR : ");
            exit(0);
    }
    fseek(fp, 0L, SEEK_END);
    size = ftell(fp);
    printf("SIZE OF FILE: %d ", size);
    printf("\n Press a key");
```

(Contd.)

```
    getchar();
    buffer = (char *) malloc(size);
    fseek(fp,0L,0);
    fread(buffer, size, 1, fp) ;
    buffer[size+1] = '\0';
    printf("\n %s", buffer);
    printf("\nPress a key");
    getchar();
    fclose(fp);
    fflush(stdin);
    printf("\n ENTER PATTERN TO WHICH WANT TO
            REPLACE: ");
    gets(pattern1);
    fflush(stdin);
    printf("\n ENTER NEW PATTERN: ");
    gets(pattern2);

    replacement(buffer, pattern1, pattern2);
    printf("\n %s", buffer);
    printf("\nPress a key");
    getchar();
}
```

Program 10.

```
/**   STRING13.C   **/

# include<stdio.h>
# include<string.h>
# include<malloc.h>
# include<stdlib.h>

void markov(char *, char *, char * );

/**            Global parameters                 **/

char *buffer;
char ch;
char pattern1[9];
char pattern2[9];

char *s;
```

(Contd.)

```
char s1[8];
int size ;
int i, j;
int length;
int l ;
int position ;
int back1, back2 ;

void main()
{
    FILE *fp ;

    fp = fopen("TEST","r");
    if( fp == NULL )
    {
            printf(" FILE \n");
            perror("ERROR : ");
            exit(0);
    }
    fseek(fp, 0L, SEEK_END);
    size = ftell(fp);
    printf("SIZE OF FILE: %d", size);
    printf("\n Press a key\n");
    getchar();
    buffer = (char *) malloc(size+1);
    fseek(fp,0L,0);
    fread(buffer, size, 1, fp) ;
    buffer[size] = '\0' ;
    printf("%s", buffer);
    getchar();
    fclose(fp);

    do
    {
            fflush(stdin);
            printf("Enter choice n for break ");
            ch = getchar();
            fflush(stdin);
            printf("\n ENTER PATTERN TO WHICH WANT TO
                    REPLACE: ");
            gets(pattern1);
```

(Contd.)

```
            fflush(stdin);
            printf("\n ENTER NEW PATTERN : ");
            gets(pattern2);

            markov(buffer, pattern1, pattern2);
    } while( ch !='n');
}

void markov(char *buffer, char *pattern1, char
*pattern2)
{
    int k, b;
    char *temp ;

    length = strlen(pattern1);
    s = ( char *) malloc(length);
    printf("\n Length = %d", length);
    back1 = length ;
    back2 = size ;
    getchar();

    i = 0 ;
    j = 0 ;
    l = 0 ;
    position = 0 ;

    while(size)
    {
            size --;
            while(length)
            {
                    position ++ ;
                    if ( buffer[i] == pattern1[j])
                    {
    if ((position >= back2) || (position < 0))
                                exit(0);
                            s[j] = buffer[i];
                            l ++ ;
                            i ++ ;
                            size --;
                            j ++ ;
                            length --;
```

(Contd.)

```
                    if( l == backl)
                    {
                            s[j] = '\0';
printf("\nPATTERN IS FOUND");
printf("\n****************\n");
printf(" LENGTH OF PATTERN  =  %d", l);
printf("\n PATTERN IS : %s", s);
printf("\n Starting Position = %i", (position-1));

/*  REPLACEMENT SECTION */

            k = 0;
            for( k = 0 ; k < (position-1) ; k++ )
                    {
            temp[k] = buffer[k] ;
                    }
                    j = 0 ;
                    b =   (k+ strlen(pattern2));

            for (  ; k < b ; k ++)
                    {
            temp[k] = pattern2[j] ;
                    j++ ;
                    }
            temp[k] = '\0';
                    getchar();
                    b = k ;
                    k = position + 1;
                    for (  ;  k < back2 ; k ++)
                    {
            temp[b] = buffer[k] ;
                    b++ ;
                    }
            temp[b] = '\0';
                    buffer = temp ;

    /* END OF REPLACEMENT SECTION */

                    l= 0 ;
                    j = 0 ;
printf("\nPATTERN REPLACEMENT IN PROGRESS");
printf("\n********************************\n");
```

(Contd.)

```
printf("\nSEE AFTER FIRST PATTERN REPLACEMENT ");

printf("\n***********************************\n");
printf("%s", buffer);

                    } /* end of if */
                    }  /* end of if */

                    else
                    {
                    i++;
                    j = 0;
                    l = 0;
                    size -- ;
                    length = back1;
                    }

            }  /* end first while */

            length = back1 ;
    }      /* end of second while */
}
```

Program 11.

```
/**    STRING2.C  **/

# include<stdio.h>

void main()
{
    char s[128][128];
    int i, j;
    char ch;
    int n,m;
    j = 0;
    i = 0;
    printf("Enter size of information in line: ");
    scanf("%d", &n);
    fflush(stdin);
    while(n)
    {
```

(Contd.)

```
            ch = getchar();
            s[i][j] = ch ;
            j++;
            if(ch == '\n')
            {
                    s[i][j]='\0';
                    printf("\n");
                    j = 0;
                    i++;
                    n--;
            }
    }
    s[i][j]='\0';
    m = i;
    printf("\nm -->%d ", m);

    /**          Display section             **/
    printf("\n");
    for( i = 0 ; i < m ; i++)
    {
           printf("\n %s\n ", s[i]);
    }
}
```

Program 12.

```
/**   STRING3.C  **/

# include<stdio.h>

int i, choice;
char ch;

void display (int, char day[7][20]);
void update_fun (int, char day[7][20]);
void draw_back ( int, char day[7][20]);

/* Output function */

void display (int n, char weak_days[7][20])
{
   printf("\n ***************************");
```

(Contd.)

```
    printf("\n RECORD No.       INFORMATION");
    printf("\n ***************************");
    for(i = 0 ; i < n ; i++)
    {
          printf("\n  %d                    %s", i,
weak_days[i]);
    }
    printf("\n ***************************");
    printf("\nPress a key");
    getchar();
}

/* Update function */

void update_fun(int n, char weak_days[7][20])
{
    printf("\nInput the record number to which want
            to update: ");
    scanf("%d", &choice);

    printf("\nYou want to update it : %s",
            weak_days[choice]);
    printf("\n Input the new value : ");
    scanf("%s", weak_days[choice]);
}

/* Draw back function */
void draw_back(int n, char weak_days[7][20])
{
    printf("\n Draw back section Update");
    printf("\n *************************");
    printf("\nInput the record number to which want
            to update: ");
    scanf("%d", &choice);
    fflush(stdin);
    printf("\n You want to update it : %s",
            weak_days[choice]);
    printf("\nInput the new value : ");
    gets(weak_days[choice]);
    ch = getchar();
    i = 0 ;
    while(ch != '\n')
```

(Contd.)

```
    {
            weak_days[choice][i++] = ch ;
            ch = getchar();
    }
}

/* Function main */

void main()
{
    char weak_days[7][20]= {
                                "MONDAY",
                                "TUESDAY",
                                "WEDNESDAY",
                                "THURSDAY",
                                "FRIDAY",
                                "SATURDAY",
                                "SUNDAY"
                                            };

    int n = 7;
    printf("\n Information List ");
    display(n, weak_days);
    update_fun(n, weak_days);
    printf("\n List after update operation\n");
    display(n, weak_days);
    draw_back (n, weak_days);
    printf("\n List after Draw back operation\n");
    display(n, weak_days);
}
```

Program 13.

```
/**   STRING4.C  **/

# include<stdio.h>
# include<malloc.h>


void gets1 (char **, int );
void display ( char **, int);
void input (char **, int );
```

(Contd.)

```
/*  gets1() function to read a string */
void gets1(char **s, int i )
{
    int j;
    char ch;
    ch = getchar();
    while(ch != '\n')
    {
            s[i][j] = ch ;
            ch = getchar();
            j++;
    }
    s[i][j]='\0';
}

/* Output funtion */

void display(char **str, int n)
{
    int i;
    printf("\nEntered strings are follows");
    printf("\n****************************");
    for(i = 0 ; i < n; i++ )
    {
    printf("\n %s", str[i]);
    }
    printf("\n Press a key");
    getchar();
}

/* Input function */

void input( char **str, int n)
{
    int i;
    int size;

    for ( i = 0 ; i < n ; i++ )
    {
            fflush(stdin);
    printf("\n Enter Approximate size of string->");
    scanf("%d", &size);
```

(Contd.)

```
            fflush(stdin);
            str[i] = (char *) malloc(size);
            printf("\n Input the string: ");
            gets1(str,i);
      }
}

/*  Function main */

void main()
{
      int n;
      char *str[50];
      printf("\n Input number of strings want to
             process:");
      scanf("%d", &n);
      input(str, n);
      display(str, n);
}
```

Program 14.

```
/**  STRING5.C **/

# include<stdio.h>
# include<string.h>
# include<malloc.h>
# include<stdlib.h>

void main()
{
      char *buffer;
      char string[] = "language";
      char *s;
      char s1[8];
      int size ;
      int i, j;
      int length;
      int l ;
      int position ;
      int back1, back2 ;
      FILE *fp ;
```

(Contd.)

```
fp = fopen("TEST","r");
if( fp == NULL )
{
   printf(" FILE \n");
   perror("ERROR : ");
   exit(0);
}

fseek(fp, 0L, SEEK_END);
size = ftell(fp);
printf("SIZE OF INFORMATION: %d", size);
printf("\n Press a key");
getchar();
buffer = (char *) malloc(size);
fseek(fp,0L,0);
fread(buffer, size, 1, fp) ;
printf("\n");
buffer[size]='\0';
printf("\n %s", buffer);
fclose(fp);
fflush(stdin);
printf("\n Input the Pattern: ");
gets(string);

length = strlen(string);
s = ( char *) malloc(length);
printf("Length => %d", length);
back1 = length;
back2 = size ;
getchar();

i = 0 ;
j = 0 ;
l = 0 ;
position = 0 ;

while(size)
{
   size --;
   while(length)
   {
      position ++ ;
```

(Contd.)

```
        if ( buffer[i] == string[j])
        {
        if ((position >= back2) || (position < 0))
              exit(0);
           s[j] = buffer[i];
           l ++ ;
           i ++ ;
           size --;
           j ++ ;
           length --;
           if( l == back1)
           {
              s[j] = '\0';
printf("\n Pattern is found\n");
printf(" Length of pattern: %d and Pattern is
        : %s ", l, s);
printf("\n Starting Position -> %d", (position-1));
printf("\n Press a key");
           getchar();
           l= 0 ;
           j = 0 ;
    for(i = (position - back1); i < position ; i++)
              {
                 s1[j] = buffer[i] ;
                 j++;
              }
              s1[j] = '\0';
    printf("\nThe old pattern is as follows ");
    printf("\n******************************\n");
              puts(s1);
              fflush(stdin);
              printf("\n Enter New Pattern : ");
              gets(s1);
printf("\nThe pattern replacement in progress");
printf("\n**********************************\n");
              j = 0 ;
      for(i = (position - strlen(s1)); i < position
          ; i++)
              {
                 buffer[i] = s1[j];
                 putchar(buffer[i]);
                 getchar();
```

(Contd.)

```
                j++;
            }
        printf("\n After replacing the pattern");
        printf("\n ****************************\n");
        printf("\n %s", buffer);
            }
        }

        else
        {
            i++;
            j = 0;
            l = 0;
            size -- ;
            length = back1;
        }
    }
    length = back1 ;
    }
    fclose(fp);
}
```

Program 15.

```
/**   STRING6.C  **/

# include<stdio.h>
# include<malloc.h>

char *sub_string(char *, int , int );

void main()
{
    char string[] = "MY FATHER IS PRINCIPAL OF
G.B.P.E.C";
    char *substr;

    substr = ( char *) malloc(9);

    printf("\n INPUT PATTERN IS ");
    printf("\n *************** \n");
    printf("\n %s", string);
```

(Contd.)

```
    printf("\n\n PATTERN FOUND ");
    printf("\n ************* \n");
    substr = sub_string(string, 13, 9);
    printf("\n %s", substr);
    printf("\n Press a key");
    getchar();

}

/* This function finds the pattern */

char *sub_string(char *string, int strpos, int size
)
{
    char *substring;
    int i = 0 ;
    substring = ( char *) malloc(size);
    while(size)
    {
            substring[i] = string[strpos];
            strpos ++;
            i ++;
            size --;
    }
    substring[i] = '\0';
    return(substring);
}
```

Program 16.

```
/**    STRING7.C   **/

/** In this program segment the text    **/
/** provided through file               **/

# include<stdio.h>
# include<string.h>
# include<malloc.h>
# include<stdlib.h>

int index(char *buffer, char *string);
```

(Contd.)

```
/**          Global Parameters          **/

char *buffer;
char string[] = "language";
char *s;
char s1[8];
int size ;
int i, j;
int length;
int l ;
int position ;
int back1, back2 ;

/**               end                    **/
void main()
{
   FILE *fp;
   char file[13];

   printf("\nEnter Text File ");
   gets(file);
   fp = fopen(file,"r");
   if( fp == NULL )
   {
         puts(file);
         perror("ERROR : ");
         exit(0);
   }

   fseek(fp, 0L, SEEK_END);
   size = ftell(fp);
   printf("\n SIZE OF FILE: %d", size);
   printf("\n Press a key");
   getchar();
   buffer = (char *) malloc(size+1);
   fseek(fp,0L,0);
   fread(buffer, size, 1, fp) ;
   buffer[size+1] = '\0';
   printf("\n Enter The Pattern ");
   fflush(stdin);
   gets(string);
```

(Contd.)

```
    printf("TEXT PROVIDED IS AS FOLLOWS \n");
    printf("***************************\n\n");
    printf(buffer);
    printf("\n Press a key");
    getchar();
    fclose(fp);
    printf("\n Index value: %d", index(buffer,
            string));
}

/* Index function */

int index(char *buffer, char *string)
{
    length = strlen(string);
    s = ( char *) malloc(length);
    printf("Length: %d", length);
    back1 = length ;
    back2 = size ;

    i = 0 ;
    j = 0 ;
    l = 0 ;

    position = 0 ;

    while(size!= 0)
    {
            size --;
            while(length)
            {
                    position ++ ;
                    if ( buffer[i] == string[j])
                    {
                            s[j] = buffer[i];
                            l ++ ;
                            i ++ ;
                            j ++ ;
                            length --;
                            if( l == back1)
                            {
                                    s[j] = '\0';
```

(Contd.)

```
printf("\nPattern is found");
printf("\nSize of Pattern: %d", l);
printf("\n Pattern is : %s", s);
printf("\n Pattern Found at %d", position-back1);

                    free(s);
                    return(position-back1);
                            }
                    }
                    else
                    {
                            i++;
                            j = 0;
                            l = 0;
                            length = back1;
                    }
            }
    }
    free(buffer);
}
```

Program 17.

```
/**  STRING8.C  **/

# include<stdio.h>
# include<string.h>

void concatenate( char *, char *, char *);

void main()
{
    char str1[128];
    char str2[128];
    char output_str[257];

    printf(" Input the first string: ");
    gets(str1);
    printf("\nInput the second string: ");
    gets(str2);

    concatenate(str1, str2, output_str);
```

(Contd.)

```
    puts(output_str);
}

/* This function concatenate two strings */

void concatenate( char *s1, char *s2, char *rs)
{
    while(*s1)
    {
          *rs++ = *s1++ ;
    }

    while(*s2)
    {
          *rs++ = *s2++ ;
    }
    *rs = '\0';
}
```

Program 18.

```
/* STRING9.C */

/* Length function */

# include<stdio.h>
# include<string.h>

int length(char *p);

/* Definition of the length function */

int length(char *p)
{
    int len = 0 ;
    while(*p++)
    {
          len ++;
    }
    return (len) ;
}
```

(Contd.)

```
/* Function main */

void main()
{
    char  string[60];
    printf(" Input the string : ");
    gets(string);
    printf("Length of Input String = %i",
           length(string));
    getchar();
}
```

Link

Program 1.

```
/* CREATING CIRCULAR HEADER LINKED LIST */
/* CIRCLIST.C */

# include <stdio.h>
# include <malloc.h>

struct link
{
   int info;
   struct link *next;
};

int i; /* Represents number of nodes in the list */
int number;
struct link *start, *newl;

void insertion(struct link *);
void create_circular_list(struct link *);
void display(struct link *);


/* Function create a circular header linked list */

void create_circular_list( struct link *node)
{
   char ch;

   node = start;      /* Point to the header node
in the list */
   node->next = (struct link *)
malloc(sizeof(struct link));
```

(Contd.)

```
    i = 0;
    printf("\n Input choice n for break: ");
    ch = getchar();
    while(ch != 'n')
    {
        node->next = (struct link* )
        malloc(sizeof(struct link));
        node = node->next;
        printf("\n Input the node: %d:", (i+1));
        scanf("%d", &node->info);
        fflush(stdin);
        printf("\n Input choice n for break: ");
        ch = getchar();
        i++;
    }
    printf("\n Total nodes = %d", i);
    node = start;
    node->info = i; /* Assign total number of nodes
                       to the header node */
}

/* Inserting a node in circular header linked */
void insertion(struct link *node)
{
    int count = node->info;
    int node_number = 0;
    int insert_node;

    node = start;
    node = node->next;

printf("\n Input node number you want to insert:");
printf("\n Value should be less are equal to the");
printf("\n number of nodes in the list: ");
scanf("%d", &insert_node);

    while(count)
    {
        if((node_number+1) == insert_node)
        {
            new1 = (struct link* )
malloc(sizeof(struct link));
```

(Contd.)

```
            new1->next = node->next ;
            node->next = new1;
            printf("\n Input the node value: ");
            scanf("%d", &new1->info);
                    node = node->next;
                    count--;
            }
            else
            {
                    node = node->next;
                    count--;
            }
            node_number ++;
    }
    if (count == 0)
    {
    node = start;  /* Points to header node */
    node->info = node->info+1;
    }
}

/* Display the list */

void display(struct link *node)
{
    int count = node->info;

    node = start;
    node = node->next;

    while (count-1)
    {
            printf("\n 0x%x", node);
            printf(" %d ", node->info);
            node = node->next;
            count --;
    }
}
/* Function main */

void main()
{
    struct link *node = (struct link *)
```

(Contd.)

```
        malloc(sizeof(struct link));
        create_circular_list(node);
        printf("\n Before inserting a node list is as
              follows:\n");
        display(node);
        insertion(node);
        printf("\n After inserting a node list is as
              follows:\n");
        display(node);
}
```

Program 2.

```
/*DELETE A NODE FROM A SIMPLE DOUBLY LINKED LIST */
/* DBL_D.C */

# include <stdio.h>
# include <malloc.h>

struct Double
{
    char info;
    struct Double *next;
    struct Double *previous;
};

int num ;
struct Double start;

void Doubly_Link_Del (struct Double *);
void Doubly_Link_Creat (struct Double *);
void display (struct Double *);

/* Function creates a doubly linked list */

void Doubly_Link_Creat (struct Double *node)
{
    char ch;
    start.next = NULL;  /* Empty list */
    start.previous = NULL;
    node = &start;     /* Point to the start of
                                the list */
```

(Contd.)

```
    num = 0;

    printf("\n Input choice n for break: ");
    ch = getchar();

    while(ch != 'n')
    {
       node->next = (struct Double *)
    malloc(sizeof(struct Double));
       node->next->previous = node;
       node = node->next;
       printf("\n Input the values of the node:
    %d:", (num+1));
       scanf("%d",  &node->info);
       node->next = NULL;
       fflush(stdin);
       printf("\n Input choice n for break: ");
       ch = getchar();
       num ++;
    }
    printf("\n Total nodes = %d", num);
}

/* Function delete */

void Doubly_Link_Del (struct Double *node)
{
    int delete_node;
    int search_counter = 0;

    printf("\n Input the node number to which you
want delete: ");
    scanf("%d", &delete_node);

    node = start.next;
    if ( node == NULL)
    {
       printf("\n Underflow\n");
       printf("\n List is empty\n");
    }
    else
```

(Contd.)

```
        while(node)
        {
            if((search_counter + 1) == delete_node)
            {
            node->previous->next = node->next ;
            node->next->previous = node->previous ;
                free(node);
            }
            else
            {
                node = node->next;

            }
            search_counter++;
        }
}

/* Display the list */

void display(struct Double *node)
{
    node = start.next;

    while (node)
    {
        printf("\n 0x%x", node);
        printf("  %d", node->info);
        node = node->next;
    }
}

/* Function main */
void main()
{
    struct Double *node = (struct Double *)
    malloc(sizeof(struct Double));
    Doubly_Link_Creat(node);
    printf("\n Created linked list is as
    follows\n");
    display(node);
    Doubly_Link_Del(node);
    printf("\n After deletion of a node linked list
```

(Contd.)

```
is as follows\n");
   display(node);
}
```

Program 3.

```
/* DELETE A NODE FROM A SIMPLE DOUBLY LINKED LIST
*/
/* DBL_DF.C */

# include <stdio.h>
# include <malloc.h>

struct Double
{
   char info[20];
   struct Double *next;
   struct Double *previous;
};

int num ;
struct Double start;

void Doubly_Link_Del_First (struct Double *);
void Doubly_Link_Creat_First (struct Double *);
void display (struct Double *);

/* Function creates a doubly linked list */

void Doubly_Link_Creat_First (struct Double *node)
{
   char ch;
   start.next = NULL;  /* Empty list */
   start.previous = NULL;
   node = &start;     /* Point to the start of the
                         list */

   num = 0;

   printf("\n Input choice n for break:");
   ch = getchar();
```

(Contd.)

```
    while(ch != 'n')
    {
        node->next = (struct Double *)
        malloc(sizeof(struct Double));
        node->next->previous = node;
        node = node->next;
        fflush(stdin);
        printf("\n Input the values of the node :
        %d:", (num+1));
        gets(node->info);
        node->next = NULL;
        fflush(stdin);
        printf("\n Input choice n for break:");
        ch = getchar();
        num ++;
    }
    printf("\n Total nodes = %d", num);
}

/* Function delete */

void Doubly_Link_Del_First (struct Double *node)
{
    node = start.next;
    if( node == NULL)
    {
        printf("\n Underflow");
    }
    else
    {
        node->previous->next = node->next ;
        node->next->previous = node->previous ;
        free(node);
    }
}

/* Display the list */

void display(struct Double *node)
{
    node = start.next;
    if (node == NULL)
```

(Contd.)

```
    {
       printf("\n List is empty\n");
    }
    else
       while (node)
       {
           printf("\n 0x%x", node);
           printf(" %s", node->info);
           node = node->next;
       }
}

/* Function main */

void main()
{
    struct Double *node = (struct Double *)
    malloc(sizeof(struct Double));
    Doubly_Link_Creat_First (node);
    printf("\n Created linked list is as
    follows\n");
    display (node);
    Doubly_Link_Del_First (node);
    printf("\n After deletion of first node list is
    as follows\n");
    display(node);
}
```

Program 4.

```
/* DELETE A NODE FROM A SIMPLE DOUBLY LINKED LIST*/
/* DBL_DL.C */
# include <stdio.h>
# include <malloc.h>

struct Double
{
    int info;
    struct Double *next;
    struct Double *previous;
};
```

(Contd.)

```
int num ;
struct Double start;

void Doubly_Link_Del_Last (struct Double *);
void Doubly_Link_Creat_Last (struct Double *);
void display (struct Double *);

/* Function creates a doubly linked list */

void Doubly_Link_Creat_Last (struct Double *node)
{
    char ch;
    start.next = NULL;  /* Empty list */
    start.previous = NULL;
    node = &start;       /* Point to the start of the
                            list */

    num = 0;

    printf("\n Input choice n for break: ");
    ch = getchar();

    while(ch != 'n')
    {
            node->next = (struct Double *)
            malloc(sizeof(struct Double));
            node->next->previous = node;
            node = node->next;
            printf("\n Input the values of the node:
            %d: ", (num+1));
            scanf("%d", &node->info);
            node->next = NULL;
            fflush(stdin);
            printf("\n Input choice n for break:");
            ch = getchar();
            num ++;
    }
    printf("\n Total nodes = %d", num);
}

/* Function delete */
```

(Contd.)

```
void Doubly_Link_Del_Last (struct Double *node)
{
    num = 0;
    node = start.next;
    if( node == NULL)
    {
          printf("\n Underflow");
    }
    else
          while(node)
          {
                node = node->next;
                num ++;
          }
    node = start.next;

    while(num != 1)
    {
          node = node->next;
          num --;
    }

    /* Delete last node */

    node->previous->next = node->next ;
    node->next->previous = node->previous;
    node->next = NULL;
    free(node);
}

/* Display the list */

void display(struct Double *node)
{
    node = start.next;
    if (node == NULL)
    {
          printf("\n List is empty\n");
    }
    else
          while (node)
          {
```

(Contd.)

```
                printf("\n 0x%x", node);
                printf(" %d", node->info);
                node = node->next;
            }
}

/* Function main */

void main()
{
    struct Double *node = (struct Double *)
    malloc(sizeof(struct Double));
    Doubly_Link_Creat_Last (node);
    printf("\n Created linked list is as
    follows\n");
    display(node);
    Doubly_Link_Del_Last(node);
    printf("\n After deletion of last node list is
    as follows\n");
    display(node);
}
```

Program 5.

```
/*  INSERTING FIRST NODE IN THE DOUBLY LINKED LIST
*/
/*  DBL_IF.C */

# include <stdio.h>
# include <malloc.h>

struct Double
{
    char info[20];
    struct Double *next;
    struct Double *previous;
};

int i;
struct Double  start, *new1;
void Doubly_insertion_First (struct Double *);
void Doubly_Create_First (struct Double *);
```

(Contd.)

```
void Display (struct Double *);

/* Function create a list of five nodes */

void Doubly_Create_First (struct Double *node)
{
    int i = 0;
    char ch;
    start.next = NULL;  /* Empty list */
    start.previous = NULL;
    node = &start;      /* Point to the start of the
                           list */
    fflush(stdin);
    printf("\n Input choice n for break: ");
    ch = getchar();

    while (ch != 'n')
    {
          node->next = (struct Double *)
          malloc(sizeof(struct Double ));
          node->next->previous = node;
          node = node->next;
          printf("\n Input the value for: %d: ",
          i+1);
          gets(node->info);
          node->next = NULL;
          i++;
          fflush(stdin);
          printf("\n Input choice n for break: ");
          ch = getchar();
    }
}

void Doubly_insertion_First (struct Double *node)
{
    node = start.next;

    new1 = (struct Double *) malloc(sizeof(struct
    Double ));
    fflush(stdin);
    printf("\n Input the first node  value: ");
    gets(new1->info);
    printf("\n new1 address: 0x%x", new1);
```

(Contd.)

```
    printf("\n Node address: 0x%x", node);
    new1->next = node;
    printf("\n New1 next address: 0x%x", new1-
    >next);
    printf("\n Node previous address: 0x%x", node-
    >previous);
    new1->previous = node->previous;
    node->previous->next = new1;
    printf("\n node->previous.next: 0x%x", node-
    >previous->next);
    printf("\n Node previous address: 0x%x", node-
    >previous);
    printf("\n Node next address: 0x%x", node-
    >next);
    printf("\n new1 address: 0x%x", new1);
    node->previous = new1;
    printf("\n node->previous: 0x%x", node-
    >previous);
}

/* Display the list */

void Display (struct Double *node)
{
    node = start.next;

    while (node)
    {
          printf("\n 0x%x", node);
          printf(" %s", node->info);
          node = node->next;
    }
}

/* main function */

void main()
{
    struct Double *node = (struct Double *)
    malloc(sizeof(struct Double));
    Doubly_Create_First (node);
    printf("\n Created list is as follows\n");
```

(Contd.)

```
   Display(node);
   Doubly_insertion_First (node);
   printf("\n List after insertion of first node
   \n");
   Display (node);
}
```

Program 6.

```
/*  INSERTING SOME NODES IN THE DOUBLY LINKED LIST
*/
/*  DBL_IL.C */

# include <stdio.h>
# include <malloc.h>

struct Double {
    char info;
    struct Double *next;
    struct Double *previous;
};
int i;
struct Double  start, *new1;
void Doubly_insertion_Last (struct Double *);
void Doubly_Create_Last (struct Double *);
void Display (struct Double *);

/* Function create a list of five nodes */

void Doubly_Create_Last (struct Double *node)
{
    int i = 0;
    char ch;
    start.next = NULL;  /* Empty list */
    start.previous = NULL;
    node = &start;     /* Point to the start of the
                          list */

    printf("\n Input choice n for break: ");
    ch = getchar();

    while (ch != 'n')
```

(Contd.)

```
    {
        node->next = (struct Double *)
        malloc(sizeof(struct Double ));
        node->next->previous = node;
        node = node->next;
        printf("\n Input the value for: %d: ", i+1);
        scanf("%c", &node->info);
        node->next = NULL;
        i++;
        fflush(stdin);
        printf("\n Input choice n for break: ");
        ch = getchar();
    }
}


void Doubly_insertion_Last (struct Double *node)
{
    node = start.next;

    new1 = (struct Double *) malloc(sizeof(struct
    Double ));
    fflush(stdin);
    printf("\n Input the last node  value: ");
    scanf("%c", &new1->info);

    if (node == NULL)
    {
        printf("\n List is empty\n");
        printf("\n Insert as last node\n");
    }
    else
        while(node)
        {
            node = node->next;
        }

    new1->next = node;
    new1->previous = node->previous;
    node->previous->next = new1;
    node->next = new1;
}
```

(Contd.)

```
/* Display the list */

void Display (struct Double *node)
{
   node = start.next;

   while (node)
   {
      printf("\n 0x%x", node);
      printf("  %c", node->info),
      node = node->next;
   }
}

/* Function main */

void main()
{
   struct  Double *node = (struct Double *)
   malloc(sizeof(struct Double));
   Doubly_Create_Last (node);
   printf("\n Created list is as follows\n");
   Display(node);
   Doubly_insertion_Last (node);
   printf("\n List after insertion of last node
   \n");
   Display (node);
}
```

Program 7.

```
/*  MERGING TWO DOUBLY LINKED LISTS (ASCENDING
ORDER) */
/*  DBL_MRG.C */

# include <stdio.h>
# include <malloc.h>

struct Double
{
   int info;
```

(Contd.)

```
    struct Double *next;
    struct Double *previous;
};

int i;
struct Double  start, start1, *new1, *local;
void Doubly_insertion (struct Double * );
void Doubly_Create (struct Double * );
void Display (struct Double *);

/* Function create a list of five nodes */

void Doubly_Create (struct Double *node)
{
    start.next = NULL;  /* Empty list */
    start.previous = NULL;
    node = &start;      /* Point to the start of the
                           list */

    for (i = 1; i < 10; i += 2)
    {
        node->next = (struct Double *)
        malloc(sizeof(struct Double ));
        node->next->previous = node;
        node = node->next;
        node->info = i;
        node->next = NULL;
    }
}

void Doubly_insertion (struct Double *node)
{
    struct Double *new1;
    start1.next = NULL;  /* Empty list */
    start1.previous = NULL;
    new1 = &start1;        /* Point to the start of
                              the list */

    for (i = 2; i <= 10; i += 2)
    {
        new1->next = (struct Double *)
malloc(sizeof(struct Double ));
        new1->next->previous = new1;
```

(Contd.)

```
        new1= new1->next;
        new1->info = i;
        new1->next = NULL;
    }

    new1 = start1.next;
    printf("\n Second list is as follows");
    while(new1)
    {
        printf("\n 0x%x", new1);
        printf(" %d", new1->info);
        new1 = new1->next;
    }
    new1 = start1.next;

    while(new1)
    {
        int found = 0;
        local = (struct Double *)
        malloc(sizeof(struct Double));
        local = new1;
        new1 = new1->next;

        node = start.next;

        do
        {
            if ( node->info > local->info )
            {
                local->next = node;
                local->previous = node->previous;
                node->previous->next = local;
                node->previous = local;
                found = 1;
                break;
            }
            else
                node = node->next;
        } while ((node->next) && (! found));

        if (! found)
            if (node->info> local->info)
```

(Contd.)

```
            {
                local->next = node;
                local->previous = node->previous;
                node->previous->next = local;
                node->previous = local;
            }
            else
            {
                local->next = NULL;
                local->previous = node;
                node->next = local;
            }
        }
}

/* Display the list */

void Display (struct Double *node)
{
    node = start.next;

    while (node)
    {
        printf("\n 0x%x", node);
        printf(" %d", node->info);
        node = node->next;
    }
}

/* Function main */

void main()
{
    struct Double *node = (struct Double *)
    malloc(sizeof(struct Double));
    Doubly_Create (node);
    printf("\n First list is as follows\n");
    Display (node);
    Doubly_insertion (node);
    printf("\n List after merging above two lists
    (Ascending order)\n");
    Display (node);
}
```

Program 8.

```
/* CREATING A SIMPLE DOUBLY LINKED LIST */
/* DBLINK.C */

# include <stdio.h>
# include <malloc.h>

struct Double
{
   int info;
   struct Double *next;
   struct Double *previous;
};

int num ;
struct Double start;
void Doubly_link_list (struct Double *);
void display (struct Double *);

/* Function creates a simple doubly linked list */

void Doubly_link_list(struct Double *node)
{
   char ch;
   start.next = NULL;  /* Empty list */
   start.previous = NULL;
   node = &start;      /* Point to the start of the
                          list */
   num = 0;
   printf("\n Input choice n for break: ");
   ch = getchar();

   while( ch != 'n')
   {
      node->next = (struct Double *)
      malloc(sizeof(struct Double));
      node->next->previous = node;
      node = node->next;
      printf("\n Input the values of the node :
```

(Contd.)

```
        %d: ", (num+1));
        scanf("%d", &node->info);
        node->next = NULL;
        fflush(stdin);
        printf("\n Input choice n for break: ");
        ch = getchar();
        num ++;
    }
    printf("\n Total nodes = %d", num);
}

/* Display the list */

void display (struct Double *node)
{
    node = start.next;

    do {
        printf("\n 0x%x", node);
        printf(" %d", node->info);
        node = node->next;
    } while (node->next);  /* Show value of last
                               node only one time */

    do {
        printf("\n 0x%x", node );
        printf(" %d", node->info);
        node = node->previous;
    } while (node->previous);
}

void main()
{
    struct Double *node = (struct Double *)
    malloc(sizeof(struct Double));
    Doubly_link_list(node);
    printf("\n Created doubly linked list is as
    follows\n");
    display(node);
}
```

Program 9.

```
/* Double_i.c */
/* Inserting nodes in a double linked list */

#include <stdio.h>
#include <malloc.h>

void main(void)
{
    int i;

    struct ListEntry {
       int number;
       struct ListEntry *next;
       struct ListEntry *previous;
    } start, *node, *new;

    start.next = NULL;  /* Empty list */
       start.previous = NULL;
    node = &start;     /*  Point to the start of the
                           list */

       for (i = 1; i < 10; i += 2)
    {
       node->next = (struct ListEntry *)
       malloc(sizeof(struct ListEntry));
       node->next->previous = node;
       node = node->next;
       node->number = 50 + i;
       node->next = NULL;
    }

    /* Display the list */

    printf("\n List before inserting nodes\n ");

    node = start.next;
    do {
       printf("%d ", node->number);
       node = node->next;
    } while (node);
```

(Contd.)

```
/* inserting some nodes in the list */

for (i = 2; i <= 10; i += 2)
{
    int found = 0;

    new = (struct ListEntry *)
    malloc(sizeof(struct ListEntry));
    new->number = 50 + i;
    node = start.next;

    do {
        if (node->number > new->number)
        {
            new->next = node;
            new->previous = node->previous;
            node->previous->next = new;
            node->previous = new;
            found = 1;
        }
        else
            node = node->next;
    } while ((node->next) && (! found));

    if (! found)
        if (node->number > new->number)
        {
            new->next = node;
            new->previous = node->previous;
            node->previous->next = new;
            node->previous = new;
        }
        else
        {
            new->next = NULL;
            new->previous = node;
            node->next = new;
        }
}

/* Display the list */
printf("\n List after inserting nodes\n ");
```

(Contd.)

```
    node = start.next;
    do {
       printf("%d ", node->number);
       node = node->next;
    } while (node);
}
```

Program 10.

```
/* Doubly linked list */
/* This program seg,ent creates a doubly linked
list then prints in forward and backword */

/* Double_l.c */

#include <stdio.h>
#include <malloc.h>

void main(void)
{
   int i;
   struct ListEntry {
      int number;
      struct ListEntry *next;
      struct ListEntry *previous;
   } start, *node;

   start.next = NULL;  /* Empty list */
   start.previous = NULL;
   node = &start;      /* Point to the start of the
                          list */

   for (i = 1; i <= 10; i++)
   {
      node->next = (struct ListEntry *)
      malloc(sizeof(struct ListEntry));
      node->next->previous = node;
      node = node->next;
      node->number = 50+i;
      node->next = NULL;
   }
```

(Contd.)

```
    /* Display the list */

    node = start.next;

    do {
       printf("%d ", node->number);
       node = node->next;
    } while (node->next); /* Show 60 only one time*/


    do {
       printf("%d ", node->number);
       node = node->previous;
    } while (node->previous);
}
```

Program 11.

```
/* filelist.c */

#include <stdio.h>
#include <dirent.h>
#include <malloc.h>
#include <string.h>
#include <stdlib.h>

void main(int argc, char *argv[])
{
   DIR *directory_pointer;
   struct dirent *entry;

   struct FileList {
      char filename[64];
      struct FileList *next;
   } start, *node;


   if ((directory_pointer = opendir(argv[1])) ==
   NULL)
      printf("Error opening %s\n", argv[1]);
   else
```

(Contd.)

```
{
    start.next = NULL;
    node = &start;

    while (entry = readdir(directory_pointer))
    {
        node->next = (struct FileList *)
        malloc(sizeof(struct FileList));
        if (node == NULL)
        {
            printf("Insufficient memory to store
            list\n");
            exit(1);
        }
        node = node->next;
strcpy(node->filename, entry->d_name);
        node->next = NULL;
    }

    closedir(directory_pointer);


    node = &start;

    while (node)
    {
        printf("%s\n", node->filename);
        node = node->next;
    }

  }
}
```

Program 12.

```
/* Sorting a directory contents with the help of
linked list */
/* L_DIR_S.C */

# include <stdio.h>
# include <dirent.h>
# include <malloc.h>
# include <string.h>
```

(Contd.)

```
# include <stdlib.h>

struct File_List
{
    char filename[64];
    struct File_List *next;
};

DIR *directory_pointer;
struct dirent *entry;

struct File_List  start, *node, *previous, *new1;

void dir_list(int k, char *l[])
{
    int number = 0;
    if ((directory_pointer = opendir(l[1])) == NULL)
    {
        perror("|ERROR\n");
        printf("\n OPENING FILE: %s", l[1]);
    }

    else
    {
        start.next = NULL;

        while (entry = readdir(directory_pointer))
        {
            /* Find the correct location */
            previous = &start;
            node = start.next;

            while ((node) && (strcmp((char *) entry,
            node->filename) > 0))
            {
                node = node->next;
                previous = previous->next;
            }

            new1 = (struct File_List *)
malloc(sizeof(struct File_List));
            if (new1 == NULL)
```

(Contd.)

```
            {
                printf("Insufficient memory to store
                list\n");
                exit(1);
            }
            new1->next = node;
            previous->next = new1;
            strcpy(new1->filename, (char *) entry);
            number++;
        }

        closedir(directory_pointer);

        node = start.next;

        while (node)
        {
            printf(" %s", node->filename);
            node = node->next;
            getchar();
        }
        printf(" Total Files listed: %d", number);
    }
}

/* Function main */
void main(int argc, char *argv[])
{
    dir_list(argc, argv);
}
```

Program 13.

```
/* LINK.C */
/* This program segment defines linked list having
a character type node */

# include<stdio.h>
# include<malloc.h>
        struct list
            {
             char data ;
```

(Contd.)

```
            struct list *next ;
        } ;

    typedef  struct list Linked;

    void main()
    {
        Linked *start, node1, node2 , node3 ,
         node4;
        int i ;
        start = (struct list *)
         malloc(sizeof(Linked));
        start = &node1;

        node1.data = 'A' ;
        node1.next = &node2;

        node2.data = 'B' ;
        node2.next = &node3;

        node3.data = 'C' ;
        node3.next = &node4;
        node4.data = 'D' ;

    for( i = 0 ; i < 4 ; i++ )
    {
          printf("\n %c", start->data);
          start = start->next ;
          printf("\nPress a key");
          getchar() ;
     }
     }
```

Program 14.

```
/* CREATING SIMPLE LINKED LIST */
/* LINK_C.C */

# include <stdio.h>
# include <malloc.h>

struct link
```

(Contd.)

```
{
   int info;
   struct link *next;
};

int i;
struct link *start = NULL; /* Shows empty list */

void creat_link_list (struct link *);
void display (struct link *);

void creat_link_list (struct link *node)
{
   char ch;
   printf("\n Input choice n for break: ");
   i = 0;
   ch = getchar();
   while(ch !='n')
   {
      printf("\n Input the node: %d :", i+1);
      scanf("%d",&node->info);
      node->next = (struct link* ) malloc (sizeof
      (struct link));
      node = node->next;
      node->next = start;
      i++;
      printf("\n Input choice n for break: ");
      ch = getchar();
   }
}

/* Display the list */

void  display(struct link *node)
{
   printf("\n Values of the entered nodes are as
   follows:\n");
   while (node)
   {
      printf("  %d", node->info);
      node = node->next;
   }
}
```

(Contd.)

```
/* Function main */

void main()
{
    struct link *node = (struct link*)
    malloc(sizeof(struct link));
    creat_link_list(node);
    display(node);
}
```

Program 15.

```
/* CREATING HEADER LINKED LIST */
/* LINK_CH.C */

# include <stdio.h>
# include <malloc.h>

struct link
{
    int info;
    struct link *next;
};

int i;
int number;
struct link *start, *new1;

void insertion(struct link *);
void create_header_list(struct link *);
void Traverse (struct link *);

/* Function to create a header linked list */

void create_header_list(struct link *node)
{
    char ch;

    start->next = NULL;  /* Empty list */

    node = start;        /* Point to the header node
                            of the list */
    node->next = (struct link* )
```

(Contd.)

```
    malloc(sizeof(struct link)); /* Create header
                                        node */
    i = 0;
    printf("\n Input choice n for break: ");
    ch = getchar();
    while(ch != 'n')
    {
        node->next = (struct link* )
        malloc(sizeof(struct link));
        node = node->next;
        printf("\n Input the node: %d: ", i+1);
        scanf("%d", &node->info);
        node->next = NULL;
        fflush(stdin);
        printf("\n Input choice n for break: ");
        ch = getchar();
        i++;
    }
    printf("\n Total nodes = %d", i);
    node = start;
    node->info = i; /* Assign total number of nodes
                        to the header node */
}
/* Inserting a node */
void insertion(struct link *node)
{
    int node_number = 1;
    int insert_node;
    int count = node->info;
    node = node->next;
    node = start;

    printf("\n Input node number you want to insert:
    ");
    printf("\n Value should be less are equal to
    the");
    printf("\n number of nodes in the list: ");
    scanf("%d", &insert_node);

    while(count)
    {
        if((node_number) == insert_node)
```

(Contd.)

```
        {
            new1 = (struct link* )
malloc(sizeof(struct link));
            new1->next = node->next ;
            node->next = new1;
            printf("\n Input the node value: ");
            scanf("%d", &new1->info);
            node = node->next;
        }
        else
        {
            node = node->next;
            count--;
        }
        node_number ++;
    }
    node = start;
    node->info = node->info+1;
}

/* Traversing the header list */

void Traverse(struct link *node)
{
    int count = node->info;
    node = start;

    node = node->next;
    printf("\n After Inserting a node list is as
follows:\n");
    while (count)
    {
        printf("\n 0x%x", node);
        printf(" %d", node->info);
        node = node->next;
        count --;
    }
}

/* Function main */

void main()
```

(Contd.)

```
{
    struct link *node = (struct link *)
malloc(sizeof(struct link));

    create_header_list (node);
    Traverse (node);
    insertion (node);
    Traverse (node);
}
```

Program 16.

```
/* DELETING FIRST NODE FROM A SIMPLE LINKED LIST */
/* LINK_DF.C*/

# include <stdio.h>
# include <malloc.h>

struct link
{
    int data;
    struct link *next;
};

int i;
int number ;
struct link start, *node, *previous;

void  Delete_node();
void  creat_node();

void creat_node()
{
    char ch;
    i = 0;

    start.next = NULL;  /* Empty list */
    node = &start;      /* Point to the start of the
list */

    printf("\n Input choice n for break:");
    ch = getchar();
```

(Contd.)

```
    while(ch != 'n')
    {
            node->next = (struct link* )
malloc(sizeof(struct link));
            node = node->next;
            printf("\n Input the node: %d: ", i+1);
            scanf("%d", &node->data);
            node->next = NULL;
            fflush(stdin);
            printf("\n Input choice n for break:");
            ch = getchar();
            i++;
    }

    node = start.next;
    previous = &start;
    printf("\n Created list is as follows\n");

    while (node)
    {
            printf("\n 0x%x", node);
            printf(" %d", node->data);
            node = node->next;
    }
}

/* Removing a node */
void Delete_node()
{
    node = start.next;
    previous = &start;

    if (node == NULL)
    {
            printf("\n Under flow");
    }
    else
    {
            previous->next = node->next;
            free(node);
```

(Contd.)

```
    }

    /* Display the list */

    node = start.next;
    printf("\n After deleting first node list is as
follows\n");
    while (node)
    {
            printf("\n 0x%x", node);
            printf(" %d", node->data);
            node = node->next;
    }
}

/* Function main */

void main()
{
    creat_node();
    Delete_node();
}
```

Program 17.

```
/* DELETING A NODE FROM A SIMPLE LINKED LIST */
/* WHEN INFORMATION OF A NODE IS GIVEN */
/* LINK_DIN.C */

# include <stdio.h>
# include <malloc.h>

struct link
{
    int info;
    struct link *next;
};

int i;
int number ;
struct link start, *previous;
void  Delete_node(struct link *);
```

(Contd.)

```
void  creat_node(struct link *);

/* Create linked list */

void creat_node(struct link *node)
{
    char ch;

    i = 0;

    start.next = NULL;  /* Empty list */
    node = &start;      /* Point to the start of the
list */

    printf("\n Input choice n for break: ");
    ch = getchar();

    while(ch != 'n')
    {
          node->next = (struct link* )
malloc(sizeof(struct link));
          node = node->next;
          printf("\n Input the node: %d: ", (i+1));
          scanf("%d", &node->info);
          node->next = NULL;
          fflush(stdin);
          printf("\n Input choice n for break: ");
          ch = getchar();

          i++;

    }
    printf("\n Total nodes = %d", i);

    node = start.next;
    printf("\n Created list is as follows: \n");
    while (node)
    {
          printf("\n 0x%x", node);
          printf(" %d", node->info);
          node = node->next;
    }
```

(Contd.)

```
}

/* Removing a node */

void Delete_node(struct link *node)
{
    int node_number = 1;
    int delete_node;

    node = start.next;
    previous = &start;

    printf("\n Input information of a node you want
to delete: ");
    scanf("%d", &delete_node);

    while(node)
    {
          if(node->info == delete_node)
          {
                printf("\n Position of the
information in the list is : %d", node_number);
                previous->next = node->next;

                free(node);
                break ;
          }
          else
          {
                node = node->next;
                previous = previous->next;
          }
          node_number++;
    }

    /* Display the list */

    node = start.next;
    printf("\n After deleting a node list is as
```

(Contd.)

```
follows:\n");
    while (node)
    {
            printf("\n 0x%x", node);
            printf(" %d", node->info);
            node = node->next;
    }
}

void main()
{
    struct link *node = (struct link *)
malloc(sizeof(struct link));
    creat_node(node);
    Delete_node(node);
}
```

Program 18.

```
/* HOW THE DIR FUNCTION  OF DOS WORK SEE IT THROUGH
LINKED LIST */
/* LINK_DIR.C */
# include<stdio.h>
# include <dirent.h>
# include <malloc.h>
# include <string.h>
# include <stdlib.h>

struct File_List
{
    char filename[64];
    struct File_List *next;
} start, *node;

void main(int argc, char *argv[])
{
    DIR *directory_pointer;
    struct dirent *entry;

    if ((directory_pointer = opendir(argv[1])) ==
NULL)
    {
```

(Contd.)

```
            perror("Error opening :");
            printf("%s", argv[1]);
    }
    else
    {
            start.next = NULL;
            node = &start;

            while (entry =
readdir(directory_pointer))
            {
                    node->next = (struct File_List *)
malloc(sizeof(struct File_List));
                    if (node == NULL)
                    {
                            printf("Insufficient memory
to store list\n");
                            exit(1);
                    }
                    node = node->next;

                    strcpy(node->filename,(char *)
entry); /* char * convert dirent to char * constant
*/

                    node->next = NULL;
            }

            closedir(directory_pointer);

            node = start.next;

            while (node)
            {
                    printf("\n %s", node->filename);
                    node = node->next;
            }
    }
}
```

Program 19.

```
/* DELETING LAST NODE FROM A SIMPLE LINKED LIST */
/* LINK_DL.C */

# include <stdio.h>
# include <malloc.h>

struct link
{
    char info;
    struct link *next;
};

int i;
int number ;
struct link start, *previous;

void  Delete_node(struct link *);
void  creat_node(struct link *);

void creat_node(struct link *node)
{
    char ch;
    i = 0;

    start.next = NULL;  /* Empty list */
    node = &start;      /* Point to the start of the
list */

    printf("\n Input choice n for break:");
    ch = getchar();

    while(ch != 'n')
    {
          node->next = (struct link* )
malloc(sizeof(struct link));
          node = node->next;
          printf("\n Input the node: %d: ", (i+1));
          scanf("%c", &node->info);
          node->next = NULL;
          fflush(stdin);
```

(Contd.)

```
        printf("\n Input choice n for break:");
        ch = getchar();
        i++;
    }

    node = start.next;
    previous = &start;
    printf("\n Created list is as follows\n");

    while (node)
    {
        printf("\n 0x%x", node);
        printf("  %c",  node->info);
        node = node->next;
    }
}

/* Removing a node */

void Delete_node(struct link *node)
{
    int node_number = 0;

    node = start.next;
    previous = &start;

    if (node == NULL)
    {
        printf("\n Underflow");
    }

    else

        while(node)
        {
            node = node->next;
            previous = previous->next;
            node_number ++;
        }
    printf("\n Total Nodes = %d", node_number);

    node = start.next;
```

(Contd.)

```
    previous = &start;

    while(node_number != 1)
    {
            node = node->next;
            previous = previous->next;
            node_number --;
    }
    if(node_number == 1)
    {
            previous->next = node->next;
            free(node);
    }
    /* Display the list */

    node = start.next;
    printf("\n After deleting last node list is as
follows\n");
    while (node)
    {
            printf("\n 0x%x", node);
            printf(" %c", node->info);
            node = node->next;
    }
}

/* Function main */

void main()
{
    struct link *node = (struct link *)
malloc(sizeof(struct link));
    creat_node(node);
    Delete_node(node);
}
```

Program 20.

```
/* DELETING A NODE FROM A SIMPLE LINKED LIST */
/* LINK_DN.C */

# include <stdio.h>
```

(Contd.)

```
# include <malloc.h>

struct link
{
    char info[20];
    struct link *next;
};

int i;
int number ;
struct link start, *previous;
void  Delete_node(struct link *);
void  creat_node(struct link *);

/* Create linked list */

void creat_node(struct link *node)
{
    char ch;

    i = 0;

    start.next = NULL;
    // Empty list
        node = &start;
    // Point to the start of the list

        printf("\n Input choice n for break: ");
    ch = getchar();

    while(ch != 'n')
    {
          node->next = (struct link* )
malloc(sizeof(struct link));
          node = node->next;
          fflush(stdin);
          printf("\n Input the node: %d: ", i+1);
          gets(node->info);
          node->next = NULL;

          printf("\n Input choice n for break: ");
          ch = getchar();
```

(Contd.)

```
        i++;
    }
    printf("\n Total nodes = %d", i);

    node = start.next;
    printf("\n Created list is as follows:\n");
    while (node)
    {
        printf("\n 0x%x", node);
        printf(" %s", node->info);
        node = node->next;
    }
}

/* Removing a node */

void Delete_node(struct link *node)
{
    int node_number = 1;
    int delete_node;
    node = start.next;
    previous = &start;
    printf("\n Input node number you want to
delete:");
    scanf(" %d", &delete_node);

    while(node)
    {
        if((node_number) == delete_node)
        {
            previous->next = node->next;
            free(node);
            break ;
        }
        else
        {
            node = node->next;
            previous = previous->next;
        }
        node_number ++;
    }
```

(Contd.)

```
    /* Display the list */

    node = start.next;
    printf("\n After deleting a node list is as
follows:\n");
    while (node)
    {
           printf("\n 0x%x", node);
           printf(" %s", node->info);
           node = node->next;
    }
}

/* Function main */

void main()
{
    struct link *node = (struct link *)
malloc(sizeof(struct link));
    creat_node(node);
    Delete_node(node);
}
```

Program 21.

```
/* SEARCH A NODE INTO A SIMPLE LINKED LIST WHEN
INFORMATION IS KNOWN */
/* LINK_HEA.C */

# include <stdio.h>
# include <malloc.h>

struct link
{
        int info;
        struct link *next;
};

int i;
int number;
struct link start, *previous, *new1;
```

(Contd.)

```
void search(struct link *);
void create_list(struct link *);
void display(struct link *);
void insertion(struct link *node);
void insertion_last(struct link *node);
void Delete_node( struct link *);

/* Function create a linked list */

void create_list(struct link *node)
{
        char ch;
        start.next = NULL;  /* Empty list */
        node = &start;      /* Point to the start
                               of the list */

        /* Create a header node that is simply
           first node in the list */

        node->next = (struct link* )
malloc(sizeof(struct link));

     /* Creattion of linked list start from here */
        number = 0;
        printf("\n Input choice n for break: ");
        ch = getchar();
        while(ch != 'n')
        {
                node->next = (struct link* )
malloc(sizeof(struct link));
              node = node->next;
              printf("\n Input the node: %d: ",
              number+1);
              scanf("%d", &node->info);
              node->next = NULL;
              fflush(stdin);
              printf("\n Input choice n for break:");
                ch = getchar();
                number++;
        }
       printf("\n Total nodes = %d",  number);
```

(Contd.)

```
        /* Create header node */

           node = &start;
           /* Point to the start of the list */
           node->info = number; /* Copy number of
           nodes in list, into the header node */
}

/* Searching a value */

void search(struct link *node)
{
        int node_number = 1;
        int search_node;
        int flag = 0;
        node = &start;
        previous = &start;

        printf("\n Input information of a node we
        want to search:");
        scanf("%d", &search_node);
        if (node == NULL)
         {
                printf("\n List is empty");
         }

        /*  By pass header node*/

        node = node->next;
        previous= previous->next;

        while(node)
         {
                if( search_node == node->info )
                 {
    printf("\n Search is successful");
    printf("\n Information to which we want search
    is: %d", search_node);
    printf("\n Position from beginning of the list:
    %d", node_number);
             node = node->next;
             previous= previous->next;
```

(Contd.)

```
                    flag = 1;
                }
                else
                {
                    node = node->next;
                    previous= previous->next;
                }
                node_number ++;
            }
            if(!flag)
            {
        printf("\n Search is unsuccessful");
        printf("\n Information·does not found in the
        list: ", search_node);
            }
}

/* Display the list */

void display(struct link *node)
{
        int count;
        node = &start;  /*start.next; */
        count = node->info;
        node = node->next;
        while (count)
        {
            printf("\n 0x%x", node);
            printf(" %d",  node->info);
            node = node->next;
            count --;
        }
}

/* Inserting a node */

void insertion(struct link *node)
{
        int node_number = 0;
        int insert_node;
        node = start.next;
        previous = &start;
```

(Contd.)

```
printf("\n Input node number you want to
insert:");
printf("\n Value should be less are equalto
the");
printf("\n number of nodes in the list: ");
scanf("%d", &insert_node);

      while(node)
      {
       if((node_number+1) == insert_node)
          {
            new1 = (struct link* )
            malloc(sizeof(struct link));
            new1->next = node ;
            previous->next = new1;
            printf("\n Input the node value:");
            scanf("%d", &new1->info);
            node = &start;
            node->info = node->info+1;
            break ;
          }
            else
             {
                node = node->next;
                previous= previous->next;
             }
            node_number ++;
      }
}

/* Function main */
void main()
{
     struct link *node = (struct link *)
     malloc(sizeof(struct link));

     create_list(node);
     display(node);
     search(node);
     insertion(node);
     display(node);
}
```

Program 22.

```
/* INSERT A NODE INTO A SIMPLE LINKED LIST AT THE
BEGINNING */
/* LINK_IF.C */

# include <stdio.h>
# include <malloc.h>

struct link
{
  int info;
  struct link *next;
};
int i;
int number;
struct link start, *previous, *new1;

void insertion(struct link *);
void create_list(struct link *);
void display(struct link *);

/* Function create a linked list */

void create_list(struct link *node)
{

  char ch;
  start.next = NULL;
  // Empty list */

      node = &start;
                /* Point to the start of the list */
  i = 0;
  fflush(stdin);
  printf("\n Input choice n for break: ");
  ch = getchar();
  while(ch != 'n')
  {
    node->next = (struct link* )
    malloc(sizeof(struct link));
    node = node->next;
```

(Contd.)

```
    printf("\n Input the node: %d: ", (i+1));
    scanf("%d", &node->info);
    node->next = NULL;
    fflush(stdin);
    printf("\n Input choice n for break: ");
    ch = getchar();
    i++;
  }
}

/* Inserting a node */

void insertion(struct link *node)
{
  node = start.next;

  previous = &start;

  new1 = (struct link* ) malloc(sizeof(struct
  link));
  new1->next = node ;
  previous->next = new1;
  printf("\n Input the fisrt node value: ");
  scanf("%d", &new1->info);
}

/* Display the list */

void display(struct link *node)
{
  node = start.next;
  printf("\n After Inserting a node list is as
  follows:\n");
  while (node)
  {
    printf("\n 0x%x", node);
    printf(" %d", node->info);
    node = node->next;
  }
}

/* Function main */
```

(Contd.)

```
void main()
{
  struct link *node = (struct link *)
  malloc(sizeof(struct link));

  create_list(node);
  insertion(node);
  display(node);
}
```

Program 23.

```
/*  INSERT A NODE INTO A SIMPLE LINKED LIST AT THE
    END OF THE LIST */
/* LINK_IL.C */
# include <stdio.h>
# include <malloc.h>

struct link
{
  char info[20];
  struct link *next;
};

int i;
int number;
struct link start, *previous, *new1;

void insertion(struct link *);
void create_list(struct link *);
void display(struct link *);

/* Function create a linked list */

void create_list(struct link *node)
{
  char ch;
  start.next = NULL;  /* Empty list */

  node = &start;  /* Point to the start of the list */
  i = 0;
  printf("\n Input choice n for break: ");
```

(Contd.)

```
  ch = getchar();
  while(ch != 'n')
  {
    node->next = (struct link* )
    malloc(sizeof(struct link));
    node = node->next;
    printf("\n Input the node: %d: ", (i+1));
    gets(node->info);
    node->next = NULL;
    fflush(stdin);
    printf("\n Input choice n for break: ");
    ch = getchar();
    fflush(stdin);
    i++;
  }
}
/* Inserting a node */
void insertion(struct link *node)
{
  node = start.next;
  previous = &start;

  while(node)
  {
    node = node->next;
    previous= previous->next;
  }
  if(node == NULL)
  {
    new1 = (struct link* ) malloc(sizeof(struct
    link));
    new1->next = node ;
    previous->next = new1;
    printf("\n Input the last node value: ");
    gets(new1->info);
  }
}

/* Display the list */

void display(struct link *node)
{
```

(Contd.)

```
  node = start.next;

  while (node)
  {
    printf("\n 0x%x", node);
    printf(" %s", node->info);
    node = node->next;
  }
}

/* Function main */

void main()
{
  struct link *node = (struct link *)
  malloc(sizeof(struct link));

  create_list(node);
  printf("\n Created list is as follows:\n");
  display(node);
  insertion(node);
  printf("\n After Inserting a node list is as
  follows:\n");
  display(node);
}
```

Program 24.

```
/* INSERT A NODE INTO A SIMPLE LINKED LIST */
/* LINK_IN.C */

# include <stdio.h>
# include <malloc.h>

struct link
{
  int info;
  struct link *next;
};

int i;
int number;
```

(Contd.)

```
struct link start, *previous, *new1;

void insertion(struct link *);
void create_list(struct link *);
void display(struct link *);

/* Function create a linked list */

void create_list(struct link *node)
{
  char ch;
  start.next = NULL;  /* Empty list */

  node = &start;      /* Point to the start of the
                         list */
  i = 0;
  printf("\n Input choice n for break: ");
  ch = getchar();
  while(ch != 'n')
  {
    node->next = (struct link* )
    malloc(sizeof(struct link));
    node = node->next;
    printf("\n Input the node: %d: ", (i+1));
    scanf("%d", &node->info);
    node->next = NULL;
    fflush(stdin);
    printf("\n Input choice n for break: ");
    ch = getchar();
    i++;
  }
  printf("\n Total nodes = %d", i);
}

/* Inserting a node */

void insertion(struct link *node)
{
  int node_number = 0;
  int insert_node;
  node = start.next;
  previous = &start;
```

(Contd.)

```
  printf("\n.Input node number you want to
  insert:");
  printf("\n Value should be less are equalto
  the");
  printf("\n number of nodes in the list: ");
  scanf("%d", &insert_node);

  while(node)
  {
    if((node_number+1) == insert_node)
    {
      new1 = (struct link* ) malloc(sizeof(struct
      link));
      new1->next = node ;
      previous->next = new1;
      printf("\n Input the node value: ");
      scanf("%d", &new1->info);
      break ;
    }
    else
    {
      node = node->next;
      previous= previous->next;
    }
    node_number ++;
  }
}

/* Display the list */

void display(struct link *node)
{
  node = start.next;

  while (node)
  {
    printf("\n 0x%x", node);
    printf(" %d", node->info).
    node = node->next;
  }
}
/* Function main */
```

(Contd.)

```
void main()
{
  struct link *node = (struct link *)
  malloc(sizeof(struct link));

  create_list(node);

  printf("\n Created list is as follows:\n");
  display(node);

  insertion(node);
  printf("\n After Inserting a node list is as
  follows:\n");
  display(node);
}
```

Program 25.

```
/*  INSERT A NODE INTO A SIMPLE LINKED LIST
    INFORMATION IS KNOWN
   AND PUT AFTER SOME SPECIFIED NODE */
/* LINK_INI.C */

# include <stdio.h>
# include <malloc.h>

struct link
{
  int info;
  struct link *next;
};

int i;
int number;
struct link start, *previous, *new1;

void insertion(struct link *);
void create_list(struct link *);
void display(struct link *);

/* Function create a linked list */
```

(Contd.)

```
void create_list(struct link *node)
{
  char ch;
  start.next = NULL;  /* Empty list */

  node = &start;
           /* Point to the start of the list */
  i = 0;
  printf("\n Input choice n for break: ");
  ch = getchar();
  while(ch != 'n')
  {
    node->next = (struct link* )
    malloc(sizeof(struct link));
    node = node->next;
    printf("\n Input the node: %d: ", i+1);
    scanf("%d", &node->info);
    node->next = NULL;
    fflush(stdin);
    printf("\n Input choice n for break: ");
    ch = getchar();
    i++;
  }
  printf("\n Total nodes = %d", i);
}

/* Inserting a node */
void insertion(struct link *node)
{
  int node_number = 0;
  int insert_node;

  node = start.next;
  previous = &start;

  printf("\n Input value node the node you want to
  insert:");
  scanf("%d", &insert_node);

  while(node)
  {
    if(node->info < insert_node)
```

(Contd.)

```
    {
      new1 = (struct link* ) malloc(sizeof(struct
      link));
      new1->next = node;
      previous->next = new1;
      new1->info = insert_node;
      break ;
    }
    else
    {
      node = node->next;
      previous= previous->next;
    }
    node_number ++;
  }
}

/* Display the list */

void display(struct link *node)
{
  node = start.next;

  while (node)
  {
    printf("\n 0x%x", node);
    printf(" %d", node->info);
    node = node->next;
  }
}

void main()
{
  struct link *node = (struct link *)
  malloc(sizeof(struct link));
  create_list(node);

  printf("\n Created list is as follows:\n");
  display(node);

  insertion(node);
```

(Contd.)

```
  printf("\n After Inserting a node list is as
  follows:\n");
  display(node);
}
```

Program 26.

```
/* LINK_N.C */
/* This program segment define linked list having
string type node */

# include<stdio.h>
# include<malloc.h>

struct list
{
  char data[30];
  struct list *next ;
};

typedef  struct list linked;

void main()
{
  linked *start, node1, node2 , node3 , node4;
  int i ;

  start = (struct list *) malloc(sizeof(linked));
  start = &node1;

  gets(node1.data);

  node1.next = &node2;

  gets(node2.data) ;
  node2.next = &node3;

  gets(node3.data) ;
  node3.next = &node4;
  gets(node4.data);

  node4.next = '\0' ;
```

(Contd.)

```
  printf("\n Output is\n");
  do
  {
    printf("\n %s",start->data);
    printf("\n Press a key");
    getchar() ;
    start = start->next ;
  } while(start->next!='\0');
}
```

Program 27.

```
/* SEARCH A NODE INTO A SIMPLE LINKED LIST WITH
INFORMATION IS KNOWN */
/* LINK_RD.C */

# include <stdio.h>
# include <malloc.h>

struct link
{
  int info;
  struct link *next;
};

int i;
int number;
struct link start, *previous, *new1;

void search(struct link *);
void create_list(struct link *);
void display(struct link *);

/* Function create a linked list */

void create_list(struct link *node)
{
  char ch;
  start.next = NULL;  /* Empty list */

  node = &start;  /* Point to the start of the list */
  i = 0;
```

(Contd.)

```
  printf("\n Input choice n for break: ");
  ch = getchar();
  while(ch != 'n')
  {
    node->next = (struct link* )
    malloc(sizeof(struct link));
    node = node->next;
    printf("\n Input the node: %d: ", i+1);
    scanf("%d", &node->info);
    node->next = NULL;
    fflush(stdin);
    printf("\n Input choice n for break: ");
    ch = getchar();
    i++;
  }
  printf("\n Total nodes = %d", i);
}

/* Display the list */

void display(struct link *node)
{
  node = start.next;
  while (node)
  {
    printf("\n 0x%x", node);
    printf(" %d", node->info);
    node = node->next;
  }
}
/* Function main */

void main()
{
  struct link *node = (struct link *)
  malloc(sizeof(struct link));
  create_list(node);
  printf("\n List in which we have to search\n");
  display(node);
  search (node);
  printf("\n List after removal of duplicate
  elements from the list\n      ");
```

(Contd.)

```
  display(node);
}

/* Searching a value */

void search(struct link *node)
{
        int node_number = 1;
        int search_node;
        int flag = 0;
        node = &start;
        previous = &start;

        printf("\n Input information of a node we
        want to search:");
        scanf("%d", &search_node);
        if (node == NULL)
          {
             printf("\n List is empty");
          }

         /*  By pass header node*/

         node = node->next;
         previous= previous->next;

         while(node)
          {
            if( search_node == node->info )
               {
                 printf("\n Search is successful");
                 printf("\n Information to which we
                 want search is: %d", search_node);
                 printf("\n Position from beginning of
                 the list: %d", node_number);
                 node = node->next;
                 previous= previous->next;
                 flag = 1;
               }
               else
                 {
```

(Contd.)

```
                        node = node->next;
                        previous= previous->next;
                    }
                    node_number ++;
            }
            if(!flag)
            {
              printf("\n Search is unsuccessful");
             printf("\n Information does not found in
              the list: %i", search_node);
            }
    }
```

Program 28.

```
/* REVERSING A LINKED LIST */
/* LINK_REV.C */

#include <stdio.h>
#include <malloc.h>

struct link
{
  int data;
  struct link *next;
};

int i, number;
struct link *start, *node, *previous, *current1,
*counter;

void display(struct link *);
void create_list(struct link *);
struct link * reverse(struct link *);

/* Reversing the list */

struct link * reverse(struct link *start)
{
  current1 = start;
  previous = NULL ;
```

(Contd.)

```
  while( current1 != NULL )
  {
    counter = (struct link *)malloc(sizeof(struct
    link));
    counter = current1->next ;
    current1->next = previous ;
    previous = current1 ;
    current1 = counter;
  }

  start = previous;
  return(start);
}

/* Definition of the function */

void  display(struct link *node)
{
  while (node != NULL)
  {
    printf(" %d", node->data);
    node = node->next;
  }
}

/* Definition of the function */

void create_list(struct link *node)
{
  int i;
  int number;

  printf("\n Input the number of nodes you want to
  create:");
  scanf("%d", &number);

  /* CREATE A LINKED LIST */

  for (i = 0; i < number ; i++)
  {
    printf("\n Input the node: %d: ", i+1);
    scanf("%d", &node->data);
```

(Contd.)

```
    node->next = (struct link* )
    malloc(sizeof(struct link));
    if( i == number - 1)
      node->next = NULL;
    else
      node = node->next;
  }
  node->next = NULL;
}

/* End of function creation */

/* Function main */

void main()
{
  struct link *node;
  struct link *p;

  node = (struct link *) malloc(sizeof(struct
  link));
  create_list(node);
  printf("\n Original List is as follows:\n");
  display(node);
  p = ( struct link *)malloc(sizeof(struct link));
  p = reverse(node);
  printf("\n After reverse operation list is as
  follows:\n");
  display(p);
}
```

Program 29.

```
/* SEARCH A NODE INTO A SIMPLE LINKED LIST WITH
INFORMATION IS KNOWN */
/* LINK_S.C */

# include <stdio.h>
# include <malloc.h>

struct link
{
```

(Contd.)

```
  int info;
  struct link *next;
};

int i;
int number;
struct link start, *new1;

void search(struct link *);
void create_list(struct link *);
void display(struct link *);

/* Function create a linked list */


void create_list(struct link *node)
{
  char ch;
  start.next = NULL;  /* Empty list */

  node = &start;      /* Point to the start of the
                         list */
  i = 0;
  printf("\n Input choice n for break: ");
  ch = getchar();
  while(ch != 'n')
  {
    node->next = (struct link* )
    malloc(sizeof(struct link));

    printf("\n Input the node: %d: ", (i+1));
    scanf("%d", &node->info);
    node = node->next;
    node->next = NULL;
    fflush(stdin);
    printf("\n Input choice n for break: ");
    ch = getchar();
    i++;
  }
  printf("\n Total nodes = %d", i);
}
```

(Contd.)

```
/* Inserting a node */
void search(struct link *node)
{
  int node_number = 0;
  int search_node;
  int flag = 0;
  node = &start ;

  printf("\n Input information of a node we want to
  search:");
  scanf("%d", &search_node);
  if (node == NULL)
  {
    printf("\n List is empty");
  }
  while(node)
  {
    if( search_node == node->info )
    {
      printf("\n Search is successful");
      printf("\n Information to which w want search
      is: %d", search_node);
      printf("\n Position from beginning of the
      list: %d", node_number+1);
      node = node->next;
      flag = 1;
    }
    else
    {
      node = node->next;
    }
    node_number ++;
  }
  if(!flag)
  {
    printf("\n Search is unsuccessful");
    printf("\n Information does not found in the
    list: %d", search_node);
  }
}

/* Display the list */
```

(Contd.)

```
void display(struct link *node)
{
 node = &start;
 while (node->next)
 {
  printf("\n 0x%x", node);
  printf(" %d", node->info);
  node = node->next;
 }
}

/* Function main */

void main()
{
 struct link *node = (struct link *)
 malloc(sizeof(struct link));
 create_list(node);
 printf("\n List in which we have to search\n");
 display(node);
 search (node);
}
```

Program 30.

```
/* CONCATENATE TWO LINKED LIST */
/* LINKCAT.C */

#include <stdio.h>
#include <malloc.h>

struct link
{
 int data;
 struct link *next;
};

struct link *start, *node;
struct link *list_one, *list_two, *list_three;

void  display(struct link *);
void  create_list(struct link *);
```

(Contd.)

```
void  link_concat_list(struct link *, struct link
*, struct link *);

void display(struct link *node)
{
  while (node->next)
  {
    printf(" %d",  node->data);
    node = node->next;
  }
}

/* Definition of the function */

void create_list(struct link *node)
{
  int i = 0;
  char ch;

  printf("\n Input choice n for break: ");
  ch = getchar();

  /* CREATE A LINKED LIST */

  while(ch != 'n')
  {
    printf("\n Input the node: %d: ", (i+1));
    scanf("%d", &node->data);
    node->next = (struct link * )
    malloc(sizeof(struct link));
    node = node->next;
    node->next = NULL;
    fflush(stdin);
    printf("\n Input choice n for break: ");
    ch = getchar();
    i ++;
  }
  printf("\n Total nodes = %d", i);
}

void link_concat_list(struct link *list_one, struct
link *list_two, struct link *list_three)
```

(Contd.)

```
{
 /* Copying first list */

 while(list_one->next != NULL)
 {
   list_three->data = list_one->data;
   list_one = list_one->next;
   list_three->next = (struct link* )
   malloc(sizeof(struct link));
   list_three = list_three->next;
 }

 /* Copying second list  */

 while(list_two->next !=NULL)
 {
   list_three->data = list_two->data;
   list_two = list_two->next;
   list_three->next = (struct
   link*)malloc(sizeof(struct link));
   list_three = list_three->next;
 }
 list_three->next = NULL;
}

/* Function main */

void main()
{
  struct link *list_one, *list_two, *list_three;

/* Assign memory to link(struct) type variables */

  list_one = (struct link *)malloc(sizeof(struct
  link));
  list_two = (struct link *)malloc(sizeof(struct
  link));
  list_three = (struct link *)malloc(sizeof(struct
  link));

  create_list(list_one);
```

(Contd.)

```
  printf("\n Original list ONE is as follows:\n");
  display(list_one);

  create_list(list_two);
  printf("\n Original list TWO is as follows:\n");
  display(list_two);
  link_concat_list(list_one, list_two, list_three);
  printf("\n Original list ONE + TWO is as
  follows:\n");
  display(list_three);
}
```

Program 31.

```
/* INSERT A NODE INTO A SIMPLE LINKED LIST */
/* LINK_CIR.C */

# include <stdio.h>
# include <malloc.h>

struct link
{
  int info;
  struct link *next;
};

int i;
int number;
struct link *start, *previous, *new1;

void insertion(struct link *);
void create_list(struct link *);
void display(struct link *);

/* Function create a linked list */

void create_list(struct link *node)
{
  char ch;
  start->next = NULL;  /* Empty list */

  node = start; /* Point to the start of the list */
```

(Contd.)

```
  node->next = (struct link* ) malloc(sizeof(struct
  link));
  i = 0;
  printf("\n Input choice n for break: ");
  ch = getchar();
  while(ch != 'n')
  {
    node->next = (struct link* )
    malloc(sizeof(struct link));
    node = node->next;
    printf("\n Input the node: %d: ", (i+1));
    scanf("%d", &node->info);
    node->next = NULL;
    fflush(stdin);
    printf("\n Input choice n for break: ");
    ch = getchar();
    i++;
  }
  printf("\n Total nodes = %d", i);
  node = start;
  node->info = i;
}

/* Inserting a node */

void insertion(struct link *node)
{
  int node_number = 1;
  int insert_node;
  int count = node->info;

  node = start;
  previous = start;

  node = node->next;
  previous = previous->next;
  node = node->next;
  previous = previous->next;

  printf("\n Input node number you want to
  insert:");
  printf("\n Value should be less are equal to
  the");
```

(Contd.)

```
    printf("\n number of nodes in the list: ");
    scanf("%d", &insert_node);

    while(node)
    {
      if((node_number) == insert_node)
      {
        new1 = (struct link* ) malloc(sizeof(struct
        link));
        new1->next = node->next ;
        previous->next = new1;
        printf("\n Input the node value: ");
        scanf("%d", &new1->info);
      }
      else
      {
        node = node->next;
        previous= previous->next;
      }
      node_number ++;
    }
    if (node == NULL)
    {
      node = start;  /* Points to header node */
      node->info = node->info+1;
    }
}

/* Display the list */

void display(struct link *node)
{
  int count = node->info;

  node = previous;
  //start;
  node = node->next;
  printf("\n After Inserting a node list is as
  follows:\n");
  while (count)
  {
    printf("\n 0x%x", node);
```

(Contd.)

```
    printf(" %d", node->info);
    node = node->next;
    count --;
  }
}

/* Function main */

void main()
{
  struct link *node = (struct link *)
malloc(sizeof(struct link));

  create_list(node);
  insertion(node);
  display(node);
}
```

Program 32.

```
/* SORTING A LINKED LIST IN ASCENDING ORDER */
/* LINKSORT.C */

#include <stdio.h>
#include <malloc.h>

 struct link
   {
     int data;
   struct  link *next;
   };

 int i;
 int number ;
 struct  link *start, *node, *previous, *new1,
 *counter;

 void doubly_link_sort()
 {
   printf("\n Input the number of node we need to
   create: ");
   scanf("%d", &number );
```

(Contd.)

```
    start->next = NULL;  /* Empty list */

    node = start; /* Point to the start of the list */

   /* CREATE A LINKED LIST */

    for (i = 0; i < number ; i++)
      {
        node->next = (struct link* )
        malloc(sizeof(struct link));
        node = node->next;
        printf("\n Input the first node: %d: ",
        i+1);
        scanf("%d", &node->data);
        node->next = NULL;
      }

  /* END OF CREATION   */

   /* SORTING THE LINK LIST START FROM HERE */

      new1 = start;
      for(; new1->next != NULL; new1 = new1->next)
     {
       for(counter = new1->next; counter != NULL;
       counter = counter->next)
         {
           if(new1->data > counter->data)
             {
                 int temp = new1->data;
                 new1->data = counter->data;
                 counter->data = temp;
             }
         }
     }

 /* END OF SORTING */

   /* Display the list */

    node = start->next;
    printf("\n After sorting the list is as
```

(Contd.)

```
follows:\n");
    while (node)
      {
         printf(" %d", node->data);
         node = node->next;
      }
   }

   /* Function main */

    void main()
   {
   doubly_link_sort();
   }
```

Program 33.

```
/* SORTING A LINKED LIST IN ASCENDING ORDER */
/* LINKSORT.C */

#include <stdio.h>
#include <malloc.h>

struct link
{
  int data;
  struct  link *next;
};

int i;
int number ;
struct  link *start, *node, *previous, *new1,
*counter;

void doubly_link_sort()
{
  printf("\n Input the number of node we need to
  create: ");
  scanf("%d", &number );

  start->next = NULL;  /* Empty list */
```

(Contd.)

```
node = start; /* Point to the start of the list */

/* CREATE A LINKED LIST */

for (i = 0; i < number ; i++)
{
  node->next = (struct link* )
  malloc(sizeof(struct link));
  node = node->next;
  printf("\n Input the first node: %d: ", i+1);
  scanf("%d", &node->data);
  node->next = NULL;
}

/* END OF CREATION   */

/* SORTING THE LINK LIST START FROM HERE */

new1 = start;
for(; new1->next != NULL; new1 = new1->next)
{
  for(counter = new1->next; counter != NULL;
  counter = counter->next)
  {
    if(new1->data > counter->data)
    {
      int temp = new1->data;
      new1->data = counter->data;
      counter->data = temp;
    }
  }
}

/* END OF SORTING */

/* Display the list */

node = start->next;
printf("\n After sorting the list is as
follows:\n");
while (node)
{
```

(Contd.)

```
    printf(" %d", node->data);
    node = node->next;
  }
}

/* Function main */

void main()
{
  doubly_link_sort();
}
```

Program 34.

```
/* POLY NOMIAL WITH HELP OF LINKED LIST */
/* POLY.C */

# include <stdio.h>
# include <malloc.h>

struct link
{
  float coef;
  int expo;
  struct link *next;
};

int i;
int number;
struct link start, *previous, *new1;

void insertion(struct link *);
void create_poly(struct link *);
void display(struct link *);

/* Function create a ploynomial list */

void create_poly(struct link *node)
{
  char ch;
  start.next = NULL;  /* Empty list */
  node = &start; /* Point to the start of the list */
```

(Contd.)

```
    i = 0;
    printf("\n Input choice n for break: ");
    ch = getchar();

    while(ch != 'n')
    {
      node->next = (struct link* )
      malloc(sizeof(struct link));
      node = node->next;
      printf("\n Input the coeficient value: %d: ",
      i+1);
      scanf("%f", &node->coef);
      printf("\n Input the exponent value: %d: ",
      i+1);
      scanf("%d", &node->expo);
      node->next = NULL;
      fflush(stdin);
      printf("\n Input choice n for break: ");
      ch = getchar();
      i++;
    }
  printf("\n Total nodes = %d", i);
}

/* Display the polynomial */

void display(struct link *node)
{
  node = &start;
  node = node->next;

  while (node)
  {
    printf("+ %f", node->coef);
    printf("X^%d", node->expo);
    node = node->next;
  }
}

/* Function main */

void main()
```

(Contd.)

```
{
  struct link *node = (struct link *)
  malloc(sizeof(struct link));
  create_poly(node);
  display(node);
}
```

Program 35.

```
/* removes.c */

#include <stdio.h>
#include <malloc.h>

void main(void)
{
  int i;

  struct ListEntry {
    int number;
    struct ListEntry *next;
  } start, *node, *previous;

  start.next = NULL;  /* Empty list */
  node = &start;  /* Point to the start of the list */

  for (i = 1; i <= 10; i++)
  {
    node->next = (struct ListEntry *)
    malloc(sizeof(struct ListEntry));
    node = node->next;
    node->number = 50+i;
    node->next = NULL;
  }

  /*  Remove the number 55 */
  node = start.next;
  printf("\n List before deletion\n");
  while (node)
  {
    printf("%d ", node->number);
    node = node->next;
```

(Contd.)

```
  }

  node = start.next;
  previous = &start;
  while (node)
    if (node->number == 55)
    {
      previous->next = node->next;
      free(node);
      break;        /* End the loop */
    }
    else
    {
      node = node->next;
      previous = previous->next;
    }

  /* Display the list */
  node = start.next;
  printf("\n List after deletion \n");
  while (node)
  {
    printf("%d ", node->number);
    node = node->next;
  }
}
```

Program 36.

```
/* removes_d.c */
/* This program segment removes a node from a
doubly linked list */

#include <stdio.h>
#include <malloc.h>

void main(void)
{
  int i, found;

  struct ListEntry {
    int number;
```

(Contd.)

```
  struct ListEntry *next;
  struct ListEntry *previous;
} start, *node;

start.next = NULL;
/* Empty list */
    start.previous = NULL;
node = &start;
/* Point to the start of the list */

    for (i = 1; i <= 10; i++)
{
  node->next = (struct ListEntry *)
  malloc(sizeof(struct ListEntry));
  node->next->previous = node;
  node = node->next;
  node->number = 50 + i;
  node->next = NULL;
}

/* Display the list */

printf("\n List before deletion \n");
node = start.next;
do {
  printf("%d ", node->number);
  node = node->next;
} while (node);

/* Remove the entry */

noae = start.next;
found = 0;

do {
  if (node->number == 57)
  {
    found = 1;
    node->previous->next = node->next;
    node->next->previous = node->previous;
    free(node);
  }
```

(Contd.)

```
        else
          node = node->next;
      } while ((node) && (! found));

      /* Display the list */

      printf("\n List after deletion \n");
      node = start.next;

      do {
        printf("%d ", node->number);
        node = node->next;
      } while (node);
    }
```

Program 37.

```
/* sortlist.c */

#include <stdio.h>
#include <dirent.h>
#include <malloc.h>
#include <string.h>
#include <stdlib.h>

void main(int argc, char *argv[])
{
    DIR *directory_pointer;
    struct dirent *entry;

    struct FileList {
    char filename[64];
    struct FileList *next;
  } start, *node, *previous, *new;


  if ((directory_pointer = opendir(argv[1])) ==
  NULL)
    printf("Error opening %s\n", argv[1]);
  else
  {
    start.next = NULL;
```

(Contd.)

```
while (entry = readdir(directory_pointer))
{
  /* Find the correct location */
     previous = &start;
     node = start.next;
     while ((node) && (strcmp(entry->d_name,
     node->filename) > 0))
  {
    node = node->next;
    previous = previous->next;
  }

  new = (struct FileList *) malloc(sizeof(struct
  FileList));
  if (new == NULL)
  {
    printf("Insufficient memory to store
    list\n");
    exit(1);
  }
  new->next = node;
  previous->next = new;
  strcpy(new->filename, entry->d_name);
}

        closedir(directory_pointer);


        node = start.next;

        while (node)
        {
                printf("%s\n", node->filename);
                node = node->next;
        }
```

Recurs

Program 1.

```
/* Divide and  Conquer */
/* Find minimum and maximum from a given series of
numbers */
/* by using above said policy */

/* DIV_CON.C */

# include<stdio.h>
# define size 100

int min1, max1;
void div_con(int *, int, int *, int *);

/* definition of the function  div_con() */
void div_con( int list[], int n, int *min, int
*max)
{
    if( n == 1)
        *min = *max = list[0];
    else
        if( n == 2)
        {
            if(list[0] < list[1])
            {
                *min = list[0];
                *max = list[1];
            }
            else
            {
                *min = list[1];
                *max = list[0];
```

(Contd.)

```
                }
            }
            else
            {
                div_con(list, n/2, min,  max);
                div_con(list+ n/2, n - n/2, &min1,
                &max1);
                if( min1 < *min)
                        *min = min1;
                if( max1 > *max)
                        *max =  max1;
            }
}

/*  Function main */

void main()
{
    int i;
    int *min, *max;
    int list[size];
    int number;
    printf("\n Input the number of elements in the
    list :");
    scanf(" %d", &number);

    printf("\n Input the list elements:\n");
    for(i = 0; i < number; i++)
    {
        scanf("%d", &list[i]);
    };

    printf("\n Min and Max are :");
    div_con( list, number, min, max);
    printf("\n Mimimum = %d", *min);
    printf("\n Maximum = %d", *max);
}
```

Program 2.

```
/* FIND MAXIMUM AND MINIMUM USING ITERATIVE METHOD
*/
/* DIV_ITER.C */
```

(Contd.)

```
# include<stdio.h>

void max_min(int *, int, int , int );

/* Definition of the function  max_min() */

void max_min(int l[], int n, int max, int min)
{
  int i;
  max = min = l[0];
  for(i = 1; i < n; i++)
  {
      if(l[i] > max)
      max = l[i];
      if(l[i] < min)
      min = l[i];
  }
      printf("\n Maxmum = %d", max);
      printf("\n Minimum = %d", min);
}

/* main function */

void main()
{
  int i, list[100];
  int n, max, min;

  printf("\n Number of elements in the list :");
  scanf("%d", &n);

  printf("\n Input elements of the list:");

  for(i =0; i < n; i++)
  scanf("%d", &list[i]);
  max_min(list, n, max, min);
}
```

Program 3.

```
/* Factorial of integer number */
/* FACT.C */

# include<stdio.h>
```

(Contd.)

```
int n;
long int Factorial_num( int );
void Display( int);

/* The definition of the Factorial_num() function */

long int Factorial_num( int n)
{
  if( n == 0)
    return(1);
  else
    return(n * Factorial_num( n -1 ));
}

/* Output Function */

void Display(int n)
{
  printf("\n Factorial of : %d = %ld", n,
  Factorial_num(n));
}

/* main function */

void main()
{
  int n ;

  printf("\n Input the number of which you want to
  find factorial: ");
  scanf("%d", &n);

  Factorial_num( n );
  Display( n );
}
```

Program 4.

```
/* Fibonacci Numbers */
/* FIBO.C */

# include<stdio.h>
```

(Contd.)

```
long fibo_number(int );

/* Definition of the function Fibonacci number
generator */

long fibo_number( int n)
{
  int r;
  if(( n == 1) || ( n == 0))
    return 0;
  else
    if(n == 2)
      return 1;
    else
      return (fibo_number(n-1) + fibo_number(n-2));
}

/* main function */

void main()
{
  int n;
  int i =0;
  printf("\n Input the number for Fibonacci series,
  you want to generate: ");
  scanf("%d", &n);
  printf("\n Fibonacci Series is as follows: \n");
  while(i < n)
  {
    ++i;
    printf(" %d", fibo_number(i));
  }
}
```

Program 5.

```
/* Greatest Comman Divisor */
/* GCD.C */

# include<stdio.h>

int Greatest_Comm_Div(int , int);
```

(Contd.)

```
/* Definition of the Greatest Comman Divisor
Function */

int Greatest_Comm_Div( int n, int m)
{
  if(( n >= m) && (( n % m) == 0))
    return(m);
  else
    Greatest_Comm_Div(m, (n % m));
}

/* main function */

void main()
{
  int n, m;
  int result;
  printf("\n Input the first integer number: ");
  scanf("%d", &n);

  printf("\n Input the second integer number: ");
  scanf("%d", &m);
  result = Greatest_Comm_Div(n, m);
  printf("\n Greatest Comman Diviser of : %d and %d
  is = %d", n, m, result);
}
```

Program 6.

```
/* Tower of Hanoi problem*/
/* HANOI.C */

# include<stdio.h>

void hanoi_tower(char , char , char , int );

/* Definition of the Tower Of Hanoi generator
function */

void hanoi_tower(char peg1, char peg2, char  peg3,
int n)
{
```

(Contd.)

```
   if( n <= 0)
     printf("\n Illegal entry ");

   if(n == 1)
     printf("\n Move Disk from %c to %c", peg1,
     peg3);
   else
   {
     hanoi_tower(peg1, peg3, peg2, n-1);
     hanoi_tower(peg1, peg2, peg3, 1);
     hanoi_tower(peg2, peg1, peg3, n-1);
   }
}

/* main function */

void main()
{
  int n;
  printf("\n Input the number of disc: ");
  scanf("%d", &n);
  printf("\n Tower of Hanoi for %d DISC", n);
  hanoi_tower('X', 'Y', 'Z', n);
}
```

Program 7.

```
/* Power Function */
/* POWER.C */

# include<stdio.h>

double power_f(double, float );

/* Definition of the function power_f() */

double power_f(double a, float b)
{
  if( b == 0)
  {
    return 1;
  }
```

(Contd.)

```
 else if ( b< 0)
 {
   return( (a * power_f(a,b+1)));
 }

 else
   return( a* power_f(a,b-1));
}

/* Function main */

void main()
{
 double mantissa;
 float exponent;

 printf("\n Input the Mantissa: ");
 scanf("%lf", &mantissa);
 printf("\n Input the exponent: ");
 scanf("%f", &exponent);
 if( exponent < 0)
   printf("\n maintissa ^ exponent: %lf", 1/
   power_f(mantissa, exponent));
   else printf("\n maintissa ^ exponent: %lf",
   power_f(mantissa, exponent));
}
```

Program 8.

```
/* Power Function */
/* POWER1.C */

# include<stdio.h>
# include<math.h>

double power_fract(double, float, float );
void expo();

/* The definition of the power_fract() function */

double power_fract(double a, float b, float i)
{
```

(Contd.)

```
    if( b == 0)
    {
      return 1;
    }
    else if ( b< 0)
    {
      return( (a * power_fract(a,b + i,i)));
    }

    else
      return( a* power_fract(a,b - i,i));
  }

  /* The definition of the expo() function */

  void expo()
  {
    char str[50];
    char *pstr;
    char temp;
    int count = 0;
    char ch;
    int i = 0;
    float counter;
    float exponent;
    float mantissa;
    printf("\n Input the Mantissa: ");
    scanf("%f", &mantissa);
    printf(" Input the Exponent: ");
    fflush(stdin);

    ch = getchar();

    while( ch != '\n')
    {
      if((ch == '-') || (ch == '+'))
        count--;
      if( ch == '.')
        temp = ch;
      str[i] = ch;
      ch = getchar();
      i ++;
      count ++;
```

(Contd.)

```
  }
  str[i]='\0';
  printf("\n\n Number of digits including '.' =
%d", count);
  count = i;
  if (temp == '.')
  {
    i = 1;
    pstr = &str[0];
    while(*pstr != '.')
    {
      pstr++;
      i ++;
    }
  }
  printf("\n Number of digits including sign &
period(.) character = %d",i);
  count = count - i;
  printf("\n Number of digits after decimal point =
%d", count);
  exponent = atof(str);
  counter = 1/power_fract(10, -count,1);
  printf("\n Increment/Decrement counter = %f",
counter);
  printf("\n\n Mantissa = %f", mantissa);
  printf("\n Exponent = %f", exponent);
  if(exponent < 0)
    printf("\n\n mantissa ^ exponent = %lf", 1/
power_fract(mantissa,exponent,counter));
  else
    printf("\n\n mantissa ^ exponent = %lf",
power_fract(mantissa,exponent,counter));
}

// Function main

void main()
{
  expo();
}
```

Program 9.

```
/* RECURSION TO REVRSE A SSTRING */
```

(Contd.)

```
/* STRING_R.C */

# include<stdio.h>

void recurs_string(char * );

/* Definition of the recurs_string() function */

void recurs_string(char *string)
{
  if (*string)
  {
    recurs_string(string+1);
    putchar(*string);
  }
}

void main(void)
{
  char str[100];
  printf("\n Input a string: ");
  gets(str);
  printf("\n Reverse of the string: %s", str);
  printf("\n Reverse string is: ");
  recurs_string(str);
}
```

Sort

Program 1.

```
/* binary.c */

#include <stdio.h>

int binary_search(int array[], int value, int size)
{
   int found = 0;
   int high = size, low = 0, mid;

   mid = (high + low) / 2;

   printf("\n\nLooking for %d\n", value);

   while ((! found) && (high >= low))
   {
      printf("Low %d Mid %d High %d\n", low, mid,
      high);

         if (value == array[mid])
               found = 1;
         else if (value < array[mid])
               high = mid - 1;
         else
               low = mid + 1;

         mid = (high + low) / 2;
   }
   return((found) ? mid: -1);
}

void main(void)
```

(Contd.)

```
{
    int array[100], i;

    for (i = 0; i < 100; i++)
            array[i] = i+20;

    printf("Result of search %d\n",
    binary_search(array, 33, 100));
    printf("Result of search %d\n",
    binary_search(array, 75, 100));
    printf("Result of search %d\n",
    binary_search(array, 1, 100));
    printf("Result of search %d\n",
    binary_search(array, 1001, 100));
}
```

Program 2.

```
/* BUBBLE SORT FOR SORTING STRINGS */
/* BUB_STR.C */

# include <stdlib.h>
# include <string.h>
# include <malloc.h>
# include <stdio.h>

void bubble_sort(char *array[], int );
void display(char *list[], int);

void bubble_sort(char *array[], int size)
{
    char *temp;
    int i, j;
    for (i = 0; i < size; i++)
            for (j = 0; j < size; j++)
            if (strcmp(array[i], array[j]) < 0)
              {
                    temp =(char *)
                    malloc(sizeof(array[i]));
                          temp = array[i];
                          array[i] = array[j];
                          array[j] = temp;
```

(Contd.)

```
                }
}
void display(char *list[], int n)
{
    int i;
    for(i = 0 ; i < n; i++)
    {
        printf("\n %s", list[i]);
    }
}

void main(void)
{
    char *list[100] = {
    "MONDAY", "TUESDAY", "WEDNESDAY", "FRIDAY",
    "SATARDAY" };
    printf("\n Input list is as follows:");
    display(list, 5);
    bubble_sort(list, 5);
    printf("\n Sorted list is as follows:\n");
    display(list, 5);
}
```

Program 3.

```
/* bubble.c */

#include <stdio.h>
#include <stdlib.h>

void bubble_sort(int array[], int size)
{
    int temp, i, j;

    for (i = 0; i < size; i++)
        for (j = 0; j < size; j++)
            if (array[i] < array[j])
            {
                temp = array[i];
                array[i] = array[j];
                array[j] = temp;
            }
```

(Contd.)

```
}

void main(void)
{
    int values[30], i;
    printf("\n Unsorted list is as follows\n");

    for (i = 0; i < 10; i++)
    {
        values[i] = rand() % 100;
        printf(" %d", rand()%100);
    }
    bubble_sort(values, 10);
    printf("\n Sorted list is as follows\n");

    for (i = 0; i < 10; i++)
            printf("%d ", values[i]);
}
```

Program 4.

```
/* HEAP SORT */
/* HEAP.C */

# include<stdio.h>

void  heap_sort(int *, int );
void create_heap(int *, int);
void display(int *, int);

/*  Definition of the function */

void create_heap(int list[], int n )
{

    int k, j, i, temp;

    for(k = 2 ; k <= n;  ++k)
    {
            i = k ;
            temp = list[k];
            j = i / 2 ;
            while((i > 1) && (temp > list[j]))
```

(Contd.)

```
            {
                    list[i] = list[j];
                    i = j ;
                    j = i / 2 ;
                    if ( j < 1 )
                    j = 1 ;
            }

            list[i] = temp ;
    }
}

/* End of heap creation function */

/* Definition of the function */

void heap_sort(int list[], int n)
{
    int k, temp, value, j, i, p;
    int step = 1;
    for(k = n ; k >= 2; --k)
    {
            temp = list[1] ;
            list[1] = list[k];
            list[k] = temp ;

            i = 1 ;
            value = list[1];
            j = 2 ;

            if((j+1) < k)
            if(list[j+1] > list[j])
                            j ++;
            while((j <= ( k-1)) && (list[j] > value))
            {
                    list[i] = list[j];
                    i = j ;
                    j = 2*i ;
                    if((j+1) < k)
                            if(list[j+1] > list[j])
                                    j++;
                            else
                                    if( j > n)
```

(Contd.)

```
                            j = n ;
                    list[i] = value;
            } /* end of while statement */

            printf("\n Step = %d ", step);
            step++;
            for(p = 1; p <= n; p++)
                    printf(" %d", list[p]);
        } /* end for loop */
}

/* Display function */

void display(int list[], int n)
{
    int i;
    for(i = 1 ; i <= n; ++ i)
    {
            printf("  %d", list[i]);
    }
}

/* Function main */

void main()
{
    int list[100];
    int i, size = 13 ;

    printf("\n Size of the list: %d", size);

    for(i = 1 ; i <= size ; ++i)
    {
        list[i] = rand() % 100;
    }
    printf("\n Entered list is as follows:\n");
    display(list, size);
    create_heap(list, size);
    printf("\n Heap\n");
    display(list, size);
    printf("\n\n");
    heap_sort(list,size);
```

(Contd.)

```
    printf("\n\n Sorted list is as follows :\n\n");
    display(list,size);

}
```

Program 5.

```
/* INSERTION SORT */
/* INSERS.C */

# include<stdio.h>
# include<stdlib.h>

int key;

int  insertion_sort(int *);
// prototype
void display(int *, int);

/* Definition of the insertion sort function */

int insertion_sort(int list[])
{
  int i = 0;
  int j, k ;
  printf("\nElement to be inserted Break condition
  is -0 : ");
  scanf("%d", &key);
  printf("\n Selected Element is: %d", key);

  while(key != -0 ) /* -0 is break condition */
    {
          k = i - 1;
          while((key < list[k]) && (k >= 0))
          {
              list[k+1] = list[k];
              --k;
          }

          list[k+1] = key ;
          printf("\n List after inserting an
          element ");
```

(Contd.)

```
            for(j = 0 ; j<=i; j++)
                  printf(" %d", list[j]);

            printf("\n Element to be inserted Break
            condition is -0: ");
            scanf("%d", &key);
            printf("\n Selected Element is: %d",
            key);
            i ++;

      }
      return i;
}

/* End of the insertion sort function */

/* Definition of the function */

void display(int list[], int n)
{
      int j;
      printf("\n Final sorted list is as follows:\n");
      for(j = 0 ; j < n ; j++)
            printf(" %d", list[j]);
}

/* End of the display function */

void main()
{
      int list[200];
      int n ;

      n = insertion_sort(list);
      display(list,n);
}
```

Program 6.

```
/* Insertion sort */
/* INSERT.C */
# include<stdio.h>
```

(Contd.)

```
# include<stdlib.h>

void insertion_sort(int *, int);
void display(int*, int);

void insertion_sort(int l[], int n)
{
   int pointer, temp;
   int i, k;

   l[0] = -0;
   for(i = 1 ; i <= n; i++)
   {
         pointer = i -1;
         temp = l[i];
         while(temp < l[pointer])
         {
            l[pointer+1] = l[pointer];
            pointer --;
         }
         l[pointer+1] = temp;
         printf("Step = %d", i);
         for(k = 0; k <= n; k++)
               printf(" %d", l[k]);
         printf("\n");
   }
}

void display(int l[], int n)
{
int i;
   printf("\n Sorted list is as follows\n");
   for(i = 1; i <= n; i++)
         printf(" %d", l[i]);
}

void main()
{
   int number = 10;
   int list[100];
   int i;
   printf("\n Number of elements in the list: %i",
```

(Contd.)

```
number);
    printf("\n Unsorted list is as follows \n");

    for(i = 1; i <= number; i++)
    {
          list[i] = rand() %100;
          printf(" %d", rand() %100);
    }
    printf("\n");

    printf("\n Step wise result is as follows
    \n\n");

    insertion_sort(list,number);
    display(list, number);
}
```

Program 7.

```
/* LINEAR SEARCH */
/* lsearch.c */

# include<stdio.h>


int search;
int flag;
int  input( int *, int , int);
int list[200];

void linear_search(int * , int , int );
void display(int *, int);

/* Definition of function */

void  linear_search(int l[], int n, int element)
{
    int k;
    flag = 1;
    for(k = 0; k< n; k++)
    {
        if(l[k] == element)
```

(Contd.)

```
            {
              printf("\n Search is successful \n");
              printf("\n Element: %i Found at
              Location: %i", element, k+1);
                   flag = 0 ;
            }
    }
    if (flag)
           printf("\n Search is unsuccessful");
}

void display(int list[], int n)
{
    int i;
    for(i = 0 ; i < n ; i++)
    {
           printf(" %d", list[i]);
    }
}
input(int list[], int number, int key)
{
    int i;
    key = 30;
    printf("Input the number of elements in the
    list:");
    number = 20;
    for(i = 0 ; i < 20; i++)
    {
         list[i] = rand() %100;
    }
    printf("\n Element to be searched: %d", key);
    search = key;
    return number;
}

void main()
{
    int number, key, list[200];

    number = input( list, number, key);

    key = search ;
```

(Contd.)

```
    printf("\n Entered list as follows:\n");
    display(list,number);
    linear_search(list, number, key);
    printf("\n In the following list\n");
    display(list,number);
}
```

Program 8.

```
/* MERGE SORT */
/* merge.c */

# include<stdio.h>
# include<stdlib.h>

void merge_sort(float *, int , int , int );
void merge_pass(float *, int , int );

/* Definition of the function */

void merge_sort(float l[], int top, int size, int
bottom)
{
    float temp[1000];
    int f = top;
    int s = size +1 ;
    int t = top ;
    int upper;
    while(( f <= size)&&(s <=bottom))
    {
        if(l[f] <= l[s])
        {
            temp[t] = l[f] ;
            f ++;
        }

        else
        {
            temp[t] = l[s] ;
            s ++;
        }
        t ++;
    }
```

(Contd.)

```
    if(f <=size)
    {
          for(f = f ; f<=size; f++)
          {
                temp[t] = l[f];
                t++;
          }
    }

    else
    {
          for(s = s ; s<= bottom ; s++)
          {
                temp[t]=l[s];
                t++;
          }

    }

    for(upper = top; upper <= bottom ; upper++)
    {
          l[upper]=temp[upper];
    }

}

/* Definition of the function */

void merge_pass( float append[], int m, int n )
{
    if( m!= n)
    {
          int mid = (m+n)/2;
          merge_pass( append, m, mid );

          merge_pass( append, mid+1, n );
          merge_sort( append, m, mid, n );
    }
}

/* main function */
```

(Contd.)

```
void main()
{
    float list[1000];
    int i, n = 30;
    printf("\n Size of the list: %d", n);

    for(i = 0 ; i < n ; i++)
    {
        list[i] = (float) (rand() %100);
    }

    printf("\n Entered list as follows:\n");
    for( i = 0 ; i<n ; i++)
    printf(" %d ", (int) list[i]);

    i = 0 ;

    merge_pass(list, i, n-1);

    printf("\n Merge sorted list is as follows:\n");
    for( i = 0 ; i<n ; i++)
    printf(" %d", (int) list[i]);
}
```

Program 9.

```
/* SIMPLE MERGE SORT */
/* MERGES.C */

# include<stdio.h>
int merge_sort( int , int *, int  , int *, int * );
int bubble_sort(int , int *);

/* Definition of function */

bubble_sort(int n, int l[])
{
    int flag = 1 ;
    int i, j, k, temp;
    for(j = 0 ; j< n - 1; j++)
    {
            for(k = 0 ; k<  n - j - 1 ; k++)
```

(Contd.)

```
            {
                    if(l[k] > l[k+1])
                    {
                            temp = l[k];
                            l[k] = l[k+1];
                            l[k+1] = temp ;
                            flag = 0;
                    }
            }
            if(flag)
                    break ;
            else
                    flag = 1;
    }
    printf("\n Entered  list as  follows in");
    printf("\n Ascending order: ");
    for(i = 0 ; i < n ; i++)
    printf(" %d", l[i]);
    return 0 ;
}

/* Definition of function */

merge_sort( int n, int list_a[], int m ,
int list_b[], int result_list[] )
{
    int i = 0;
    int j = 0;
    int k = 0;
    int ch, l;
    /* Repeat the process until the elements of
list_a and list_b are exhausted */

    while((i < n) &&(j<m))
    {
            if(list_a[i] < list_b[j])
            {
                    result_list[k] = list_a[i];
                    i++;
                    k++;
            } /*  end of if statement */
            else
```

(Contd.)

```
                if(list_a[i] > list_b[j])
                {
                        result_list[k] = list_b[j];
                        j++;
                        k++;
                } /* end of if statement */
                else
                {
                        result_list[k] = list_a[i];
                        i++;
                        j++;
                        k++;
                }  /* end of else statement */
        printf("\n");
        for(ch = 0; ch < k; ch++)
        printf(" %d", result_list[ch]);

    }  /* end of while statement */

    /*  checks if size of list_a larger than list_b
     copy rest of the elements of list_a into
result_list */

    if(i <n )
    {
        for(l = i ; l <n ; l++)
        {
                result_list[k] = list_a[i];
                i++;
                k++;
                printf("\n");
                for(ch = 0; ch < k; ch++)
                printf(" %d", result_list[ch]);
        }
    }
    else
        /* checks if size of list_b larger than
list_a
         copy rest of the elements of list_b into
result_list */

        if(j < m)
```

(Contd.)

```
        {
                for(l = j; l<m; l++)
                {
                        result_list[k] = list_b[j];
                        j++;
                        k++;
                        printf("\n");
                        for(ch = 0; ch < k; ch++)
                        printf(" %d",
result_list[ch]);
                }
        }
    return (k);
}

/* function main */

void main()
{
    int list_a[100],list_b[100];
    int result[200];
    int n, m, k, i;

    printf("\n Input the number of elements of
    list_a: ");
    scanf("%d", &n);

    for(i = 0; i<n ; i++)
    {
        printf("\n Input the element: %d: ",  i+1);
        scanf("%d", &list_a[i]);
    }

    /* Sort the elements of list_a */

    bubble_sort(n, list_a);

    /* End of sorting */

    printf("\n Input the number of elements of
    list_b:");
    scanf("%d", &m);
```

(Contd.)

```
    for(i = 0 ; i< m ; i++)
    {
        printf("\n Input the element: %d: ", i+1);
        scanf("%d", &list_b[i]);
    }

    /* Sort the elements of list_b */

    bubble_sort(m, list_b);

    /* End of sorting */

    k = merge_sort( n, list_a, m , list_b, result);
    printf("\n Duplicates are : %d", m+n-k);
    printf("\n");

    printf("\n Sorted list is as follows:\n");
    for(i = 0 ; i< k ; i++)
    {
        printf(" %d", result[i]);
    }
}
```

Program 10.

```
/* quick.c */

#include <stdio.h>
#include <stdlib.h>

void quick_sort(int array[], int first, int last)
{
    int temp, low, high, list_separator;

    low = first;
    high = last;
    list_separator = array[(first + last) / 2];

    do {
            while (array[low] < list_separator)
                low++;
```

(Contd.)

```
            while (array[high] > list_separator)
                  high--;

            if (low <= high)
            {
                  temp = array[low];
                  array[low++] = array[high];
                  array[high--] = temp;
            }
      } while (low <= high);

      if (first < high)
            quick_sort(array, first, high);
      if (low < last)
            quick_sort(array, low, last);
}

void main(void)
{
      int values[100], i;
      printf("\n Unsorted list is as follows \n");

      for (i = 0; i < 20; i++)
      {
         values[i] = rand() % 100;
         printf(" %d", rand() %100);
      }
      quick_sort(values, 0, 19);

      printf("\n Sorted list as follows\n");

      for (i = 0; i < 20; i++)
      printf("%d ", values[i]);
}
```

Program 11.

```
/*  QUICK SORT */
/* Sorting an array by using Hoare's quicksort */
/* QUICK1.C */

# include<stdio.h>
```

(Contd.)

```
int quick_sort(int *, int, int, int (*p_cmp_f)(int
*,int *));
int *select_pivot(int data[], int n, int size,  int
(*p_cmp_f)(int *,int *));
void memswap(int *s, int *t, int count);

void main()
{
    int n, i;
    int list[100];
    int (*p_cmp_f)(int *, int *);
    int size ;
    printf("\n Number of elements in the list: ");
    scanf("%d", &n);

    printf("\n Input the elements: \n");
    for(i = 0 ; i < n ; i++)
    scanf("%d", &list[i]);

    printf("\n Sorted list\n");
    quick_sort(list, n, size, p_cmp_f);
    for(i = 0 ; i < n ; i++)
    printf(" %d", list[i]);
}

int quick_sort(int data[], int n, int size, int
(*p_cmp_f)(int *,int *))
{
    int *p_left, *p_right, *p_pivot;
    int lsize;

    if(n <= 1)
           return 0;
    p_left = data;
    p_right = data + ( n - 1 ) * size;

    /* find pivot and move it to the right end */
    p_pivot = select_pivot(data, n, size, p_cmp_f);
    memswap(p_pivot, p_right, size);
    p_pivot = p_right;

    /* partition */
```

(Contd.)

```
    while(p_left < p_right)
    {
            while((*p_cmp_f)(p_left, p_pivot) >= 0 &&
            (p_left < p_right))
            p_left += size ;
            while((*p_cmp_f)(p_right, p_pivot) >= 0
            && (p_left < p_right))
            p_right -= size ;

            if(p_left < p_right)
            {
                    memswap(p_left, p_right, size);
                    p_left += size ;
            }
    }

    if(p_right == data )
    {
            memswap(p_right, p_pivot, size);
            p_right += size ;
    }
    lsize = (p_right -data) / size ;
    quick_sort(data, lsize, size, p_cmp_f);
    quick_sort(p_right, n- lsize, size, p_cmp_f);
}

int *select_pivot(int data[], int n, int size,  int
(*p_cmp_f)(int *, int *))
{
    return data;
}

void memswap(int *s, int *t, int count)
{
    int temp ;
    while(count --> 0)
    {
            temp = *s ;
            *s ++ = *t ;
            *t++ = temp ;
    }
}
```

Program 12.

```
/* RADIX SORT */
/* RADIX.C*/

# include<stdio.h>
# include<malloc.h>
# include<stdlib.h>

struct node
{
    int data ;
    struct node *next;
};

typedef struct node node1;

node1 *first;
node1 *pocket[100], *pocket1[100];
void create_node(node1 *, int);
void display(node1 *);
node1 *radix_sort(node1 *);
int large(node1 * );
int numdig(int );
int digit(int , int);
void update(int, node1 *);
node1 *Make_link(int, node1 *);

/* This function create nodes and take input data
*/

void  create_node(node1 *rec, int n)
{
    int i, j, k;
    for(i = 0 ; i< n; i++)
    {
      rec->next = (node1 *)
      malloc(sizeof(node1));
      printf("\n First node value: %d: ", i);
      scanf("%d", &rec->data);
      rec = rec->next;
    }
```

(Contd.)

```
    rec->next = NULL;
}

/* Output Function */

void  display(node1 *rec)
{
    while(rec !=NULL)
    {
        printf(" %d", rec->data);
        rec= rec->next;
    }
}

/* This radix sort function */

node1 *radix_sort(node1 *rec)
{
    node1 *r, *nex;
    int poc = 0 ;
    int i, j, k;
    int larg = large(rec);
    int m = numdig(larg);

    /* These statements create pockets */

    for(k = 0 ; k < 10; k++)
    {
      pocket[k] = (node1 *)malloc(sizeof(node1));
      pocket1[k] = (node1 *)malloc(9*sizeof(node1));
    }

    /* These statements initialize pockets */

    for(j = 1; j <= m ; j++)
    {
          for(i = 0 ; i < 10 ; i++)
          {
                pocket[i] = NULL;
                pocket1[i] = NULL ;
          }
```

(Contd.)

```
            r = rec ;
            while(r != NULL)
            {
              int dig = digit(r->data, j);
              nex = r->next ;
              update(dig,r);
              r = nex;
            }

            if(r!= NULL)
            {
              int dig = digit(r->data,j);
              update(dig,r);
            }

            while(pocket1[poc] == NULL)
                  poc ++;
            rec = Make_link(poc, rec);
    }
    return(rec);
}

/* This function finds largest number in the list
*/

int large(node1 *rec)
{
    node1 *save ;
    int p = 0;
    save = rec ;
    while(save != NULL)
    {
          if(save ->data > p)
          {
                p = save->data;
          }
          save = save->next ;
    }

    printf("\n Largest element: %d", p);
    return(p);
}
```

(Contd.)

```
/* This Function finds number digits in a number */

int numdig(int large)
{
    int temp = large ;
    int num = 0 ;

    while(temp != 0)
    {
        ++num ;
        temp = temp/10 ;
    }

    printf("\n  Number of digits of the number %d is
    %d", large, num);
    return(num);
}
/* This function scarve a number into digits */

int digit(int num, int j)
{
    int dig, i, k;
    int temp = num ;

    for(i = 0 ; i < j ; i++)
    {
        dig = temp % 10 ;
        temp = temp / 10 ;
    }
        printf("  %d digit of number  %d is %d", j,
        num, dig);
        return(dig);
}

/* This function updates the pockets value */

void  update(int dig, node1 *r)
{
    if(pocket[dig] == NULL)
    {
          pocket[dig] = r ;
          pocket1[dig] = r ;
```

(Contd.)

```
    }
    else
    {
            pocket[dig]->next = r ;
            pocket[dig] = r ;
    }
    r->next = NULL;
}

/* This function create links between the nodes */

node1* Make_link(int poc , node1 *rec)
{
    int i, j, k;
    node1 *pointer;
    rec = pocket1[poc];
    for(i = poc +1 ; i< 10 ; i++)
    {
            pointer = pocket[i-1];
            if(pocket[i] != NULL)
                    pointer->next= pocket1[i];
            else
                    pocket[i] = pointer ;
    }
    return(rec);
}

/* Main function */

void  main()
{
    node1 *start, *pointer;
    int number;

  printf("\n Input the number of elements in the
  list:");
  scanf("%d", &number);

  start = (node1 *)malloc(sizeof(node1));

  create_node(start, number);
```

(Contd.)

```
    printf("\n Given list is as follows \n");
    display(start);

    start = radix_sort(start);

    printf("\n Sorted list is as follows:\n");
    display (start);
}
```

Program 13.

```
/* select.c */
/* selection sort */

#include <stdio.h>
#include <stdlib.h>

void selection_sort(int array[], int size)
{
    int temp, current, j;

    for (current = 0; current < size; current++)
        for (j = current + 1; j < size; j++)
            if (array[current] > array[j])
            {
                temp = array[current];
                array[current] = array[j];
                array[j] = temp;
            }
}

void main(void)
{
    int values[30], i;
    printf("\n Unsorted list is as follows \n");
    for (i = 0; i < 30; i++)
    {
        values[i] = rand() % 100;
        printf(" %d", rand() %100);
    }
        selection_sort(values, 30);
```

(Contd.)

```
    printf("\n Sorted list is as follows \n");

    for (i = 0; i < 30; i++)
    printf("%d ", values[i]);
}
```

Program 14.

```
/* SELECTION SORT */
/* selects.c */

# include<stdio.h>

int selection_sort(int , int *); /* Prototype */

void main()
{
    int number, list[200];
    int i;
    printf("Input the number of elements in the
    list:");
    scanf("%d", &number);
    printf("\n Number  of elements in the list is:
    %d", number);

    printf("\nInput the elements of the list\n");
    for(i = 0 ; i < number ; i++)
    scanf("%d", &list[i]);

    selection_sort( number, list);
}

/* Definition of function */

int selection_sort(int n, int l[])
{
    int min ;
    int k, index;

    for(index = 0; index< n - 1 ; index++)
    {
        min = index ;
```

(Contd.)

```
        for(k = index + 1; k < n ; k ++)
        {
                if(l[min] > l[k])
                        min = k ;
        }
        if( min != index)
        {
                int temp = l [index];
                l[index] = l[min];
                l[min] = temp ;
        }
    }

    printf("\n Entered list is as  follows:\n");
    for( index = 0 ; index < n; index++)
    printf(" %d", l[index]);
    return 0;
}
```

Program 15.

```
/* shell.c */
/* shell sort */

#include <stdio.h>
#include <stdlib.h>

void shell_sort(int array[], int size)
{
    int temp, gap, i, exchange_occurred;

    gap = size / 2;

    do {
        do {
            exchange_occurred = 0;

            for (i = 0; i < size - gap; i++)
                if (array[i] > array[i + gap])
                    {
                        temp = array[i];
                          array[i] = array[i + gap];
```

(Contd.)

```
                    array[i + gap] = temp;
                    exchange_occurred = 1;
                    }
                } while (exchange_occurred);
            } while (gap = gap / 2);
    }

void main(void)
{
    int values[50], i;

    printf("\n Unsorted list is as follows \n");

    for (i = 0; i < 50; i++)
    {
        values[i] = rand() % 100;
        printf(" %d", rand() %100);
    }
    shell_sort(values, 50);

    printf("\n Sorted list is as follows \n");

    for (i = 0; i < 50; i++)
    printf("%d ", values[i]);
}
```

Tree

Program 1.

```
/* Create AVL Binary TREE */
/* AVL_TREE.C */

# include<stdio.h>
# include<malloc.h>

# define F 0
# define T 1

struct NODE
{
    char Info;
    int Flag;
    struct  NODE *Left_Child;
    struct  NODE *Right_Child;
};

struct NODE *Binary_Tree (char , struct NODE *, int
*);
void Output(struct NODE *, int );
struct  NODE *Balance_Right_Heavy(struct NODE *,
int *);
struct NODE *Balance_Left_Heavy(struct NODE *, int
*);
struct NODE *DELETE(struct NODE *, struct NODE *,
int *);
struct NODE *Delete_Element(struct NODE *, char ,
int *);

/* Function to insert an element into tree */
```

(Contd.)

```
struct NODE *  Binary_Tree (char Info, struct NODE
*Parent, int *H)
{
    struct NODE *Node1;
    struct NODE *Node2;
    if(!Parent)
    {
          Parent = (struct NODE *)
          malloc(sizeof(struct NODE));
          Parent->Info = Info;
          Parent->Left_Child = NULL;
          Parent->Right_Child = NULL;
          Parent->Flag = 0;
          *H = T;
          return (Parent);
    }

    if(Info < Parent->Info)
    {
          Parent->Left_Child = Binary_Tree(Info,
          Parent->Left_Child, H);
          if(*H)
          /* Left branch has grown higher */
          {
     switch(Parent->Flag)
     {
     case 1: /* Right heavy */
       Parent->Flag = 0;
       *H = F;
       break;
     case 0: /* Balanced tree */
       Parent->Flag = -1;
       break;
     case -1: /* Left heavy */
       Node1 = Parent->Left_Child;
       if(Node1->Flag == -1)
       {
       printf("\n Left to Left
Rotation\n");
       Parent->Left_Child= Node1-
>Right_Child;
       Node1->Right_Child = Parent;
```

(Contd.)

```
      Parent->Flag = 0;
      Parent = Node1;
    }
    else
    {
    printf("\n Left to right
    rotation\n");
    Node2 = Node1->Right_Child;
    Node1->Right_Child = Node2-
    >Left_Child;
    Node2->Left_Child = Node1;
    Parent->Left_Child = Node2-
    >Right_Child;
    Node2->Right_Child = Parent;
    if(Node2->Flag == -1)
      Parent->Flag = 1;
      else
        Parent->Flag = 0;
        if(Node2->Flag == 1)
        Node1->Flag = -1;
      else
        Node1->Flag = 0;
        Parent = Node2;
      }
    Parent->Flag = 0;
    *H = F;
  }
 }
}

 if(Info > Parent->Info)
 {
    Parent->Right_Child = Binary_Tree(Info,
    Parent->Right_Child, H);
       if(*H)
       /* Right branch has grown higher */
       {
              switch(Parent->Flag)
              {
              case -1: /* Left heavy */
                     Parent->Flag = 0;
                     *H = F;
```

(Contd.)

```
                                        break;
       case 0: /* Balanced tree */
         Parent->Flag = 1;
         break;

       case 1: /* Right heavy */
         Node1 = Parent->Right_Child;
         if(Node1->Flag == 1)
         {
           printf("\n Right to Right Rotation\n");
           Parent->Right_Child= Node1->Left_Child;
           Node1->Left_Child = Parent;
           Parent->Flag = 0;
           Parent = Node1;
         }
         else
         {
           printf("\n Right to Left Rotation\n");
           Node2 = Node1->Left_Child;
           Node1->Left_Child = Node2->Right_Child;
           Node2->Right_Child = Node1;
           Parent->Right_Child = Node2->Left_Child;
           Node2->Left_Child = Parent;

           if(Node2->Flag == 1)
             Parent->Flag = -1;
           else
             Parent->Flag = 0;
           if(Node2->Flag == -1)
             Node1->Flag = 1;
           else
             Node1->Flag = 0;
           Parent = Node2;
         }

        Parent->Flag = 0;
        *H = F;
      }
    }
  }
    return(Parent);
}
```

(Contd.)

```
/* Output function */

void Output(struct NODE *Tree,int Level)
{
  int i;
  if (Tree)
  {
    Output(Tree->Right_Child, Level+1);
    printf("\n");
    for (i = 0; i < Level; i++)
    printf("   ");
    printf("%c", Tree->Info);
    Output(Tree->Left_Child, Level+1);
  }
}

/* Balancing Right Heavy */

struct NODE * Balance_Right_Heavy(struct NODE
*Parent, int *H)
{
  struct NODE *Node1, *Node2;

  switch(Parent->Flag)
  {
  case -1:
    Parent->Flag = 0;
    break;

  case 0:
    Parent->Flag = 1;
    *H= F;
    break;

  case 1: /* Rebalance */
    Node1 = Parent->Right_Child;
    if(Node1->Flag >= 0)
    {
      printf("\n Right to Right Rotation\n");
      Parent->Right_Child= Node1->Left_Child;
      Node1->Left_Child = Parent;
      if(Node1->Flag == 0)
```

(Contd.)

```
        {
          Parent->Flag = 1;
          Node1->Flag = -1;
          *H = F;
        }
        else
        {
          Parent->Flag = Node1->Flag = 0;
        }
        Parent = Node1;
      }
      else
      {
        printf("\n Right to Left Rotation\n");
        Node2 = Node1->Left_Child;
        Node1->Left_Child = Node2->Right_Child;
        Node2->Right_Child = Node1;
        Parent->Right_Child = Node2->Left_Child;
        Node2->Left_Child = Parent;

        if(Node2->Flag == 1)
          Parent->Flag = -1;
        else
          Parent->Flag = 0;
        if(Node2->Flag == -1)
          Node1->Flag = 1;
        else
          Node1->Flag = 0;
        Parent = Node2;
        Node2->Flag = 0;
      }
    }
  return(Parent);
}

/* Balancing Left Heavy */

struct NODE * Balance_Left_Heavy(struct NODE
*Parent, int *H)
{
  struct NODE *Node1, *Node2;
```

(Contd.)

```
switch(Parent->Flag)
{
case 1:
  Parent->Flag = 0;
  break;

case 0:
  Parent->Flag = -1;
  *H= F;
  break;
case -1: /*  Rebalance */
  Node1 = Parent->Left_Child;
  if(Node1->Flag <= 0)
  {
    printf("\n Left to Left Rotation\n");
    Parent->Left_Child= Node1->Right_Child;
    Node1->Right_Child = Parent;
    if(Node1->Flag == 0)
    {
      Parent->Flag = -1;
      Node1->Flag = 1;
      *H = F;
    }
    else
    {
      Parent->Flag = Node1->Flag = 0;
    }
    Parent = Node1;
  }
  else
  {
    printf("\n Left to Right Rotation\n");
    Node2 = Node1->Right_Child;
    Node1->Right_Child = Node2->Left_Child;
    Node2->Left_Child = Node1;
    Parent->Left_Child = Node2->Right_Child;
    Node2->Right_Child = Parent;

    if(Node2->Flag == -1)
      Parent->Flag = 1;
    else
      Parent->Flag = 0;
```

(Contd.)

```
      if(Node2->Flag == 1)
        Node1->Flag = -1;
      else
        Node1->Flag = 0;
      Parent = Node2;
      Node2->Flag = 0;
    }
  }
  return(Parent);
}

/* Replace the node at which key is found with last
right key of a left child */

struct NODE * DELETE(struct NODE *R, struct NODE
*Temp, int *H)
{
  struct NODE *Dnode = R;
  if( R->Right_Child != NULL)
  {
    R->Right_Child = DELETE(R->Right_Child, Temp,
    H);
    if(*H)
      R = Balance_Left_Heavy(R, H);
  }
  else
  {
    Dnode = R;
    Temp->Info = R->Info;
    R = R->Left_Child;
    free(Dnode);
    *H = T;
  }
  return(R);
}
/* Delete the key element from the tree */

struct NODE * Delete_Element(struct NODE *Parent,
char Info, int *H)
{
  struct NODE *Temp;
  if(!Parent)
```

(Contd.)

```
{
  printf("\n Information does not exist");
  return(Parent);
}
else
{
  if (Info < Parent->Info )
  {
    Parent->Left_Child = Delete_Element(Parent-
  >Left_Child, Info, H);
    if(*H)
      Parent = Balance_Right_Heavy(Parent, H);
  }
  else
    if(Info > Parent->Info)
    {
      Parent->Right_Child = Delete_Element(Parent-
      >Right_Child, Info, H);
      if(*H)
        Parent = Balance_Left_Heavy(Parent, H);
    }
    else
    {
      Temp= Parent;
      if(Temp->Right_Child == NULL)
      {
        Parent = Temp->Left_Child;
        *H = T;
        free(Temp);
      }
      else
        if(Temp->Left_Child == NULL)
        {
          Parent = Temp->Right_Child;
          *H = T;
          free(Temp);
        }
        else
        {
          Temp->Left_Child = DELETE(Temp-
          >Left_Child, Temp, H);
          if(*H)
```

(Contd.)

```
            Parent = Balance_Right_Heavy(Parent, H);
            }
         }
    }
    return(Parent);
}

/* Function main */

void main()
{
    int H;
    char Info ;
    char choice;
    struct NODE *Tree = (struct NODE
*)malloc(sizeof(struct NODE));
    Tree =  NULL;
    printf("\n Input choice 'b' to break:");
    choice = getchar();
    while(choice != 'b')
    {
      fflush(stdin);
      printf("\n Input information of the node: ");
      scanf("%c", &Info);
      Tree = Binary_Tree(Info, Tree, &H);
      printf("\n Tree is:\n");
      Output(Tree, 1);
      fflush(stdin);
      printf("\n Input choice 'b' to break:");
      choice = getchar();
    }
    fflush(stdin);
    while(1)
    {
      printf("\n Input choice 'b' to break:");
      printf("\n Input the key value want to
      deletedir:");
      scanf("%c", &Info);
      if (Info == 'b')
        break;
      Tree = Delete_Element(Tree, Info, &H);
      printf("\n Tree is:\n");
```

(Contd.)

```
        Output(Tree, 1);
    }
}
```

Program 2.

```
/* Binary tree traversal */
/* BT_TRAV.C */

# include<stdio.h>

struct NODE
{
  char Info;
  struct NODE *Left_Child;
  struct NODE *Right_Child;
};

struct NODE *Binary_Tree (char *, int, int);
void Output(struct NODE *, int );
void Pre_order(struct NODE *);
void In_order(struct NODE *);
void Post_order(struct NODE *);

/* Function to create an binary tree */

struct NODE *  Binary_Tree (char *List, int Lower,
int Upper)
{
  struct NODE *Node;
  int Mid = (Lower + Upper)/2;
  Node = (struct NODE*) malloc(sizeof(struct
  NODE));

  Node->Info = List [Mid];
  if ( Lower>= Upper)
  {
    Node->Left_Child = NULL;
    Node->Right_Child = NULL;
    return (Node);
  }
```

(Contd.)

```
   if (Lower <= Mid - 1)
     Node->Left_Child = Binary_Tree (List, Lower, Mid
     - 1);
   else
     Node->Left_Child = NULL;
   if (Mid + 1 <= Upper)
     Node->Right_Child = Binary_Tree (List, Mid + 1,
     Upper);
   else
     Node->Right_Child = NULL;
   return(Node);
 }

/* Output function */

void Output(struct NODE *T, int Level)
{
  int i;
  if (T)
  {
    Output(T->Right_Child, Level+1);
    printf("\n");
    for (i = 0; i < Level; i++)
      printf("   ");
    printf(" %c", T->Info);
    Output(T->Left_Child, Level+1);
  }
}

/* Pre-order traversal */

void Pre_order (struct NODE *Node)
{
  if (Node)
  {
   printf(" %c", Node->Info);
   Pre_order(Node->Left_Child);
   Pre_order(Node->Right_Child);
  }
}

/* In-order traversal */
```

(Contd.)

```
void In_order (struct NODE *Node)
{
  if (Node)
  {
    In_order(Node->Left_Child);
    printf(" %c", Node->Info);
    In_order(Node->Right_Child);
  }
}

/* Post-order traversal */

void Post_order (struct NODE *Node)
{
  if (Node)
  {
    Post_order(Node->Left_Child);
    Post_order(Node->Right_Child);
    printf(" %c", Node->Info);
  }
}

/*  Function main */

void main()
{
  char List[100];
  int Number = 0;
  char Info;
  char choice;
  struct NODE *T = (struct NODE *)
  malloc(sizeof(struct NODE));
  T = NULL;
  printf("\n Input choice 'b' to break:");
  choice = getchar();
  fflush(stdin);
  while(choice != 'b')
  {
    printf("\n Input information of the node: ");
    scanf("%c", &Info);
    List[Number++] = Info;
    fflush(stdin);
```

(Contd.)

```
    printf("\n Input choice 'b' to break:");
    choice = getchar();
    fflush(stdin);
   }
   Number --;
   printf("\n Number of elements in the list is %d",
   Number);
   T = Binary_Tree(List, 0, Number);
   Output(T,1);
   printf("\n Pre-order traversal\n");
   Pre_order (T);
   printf("\n In-order traversal\n");
   In_order (T);
   printf("\n Post-order traversal\n");
   Post_order (T);
}
```

Program 3.

```
/* Create Binary TREE */
/* CREAT_BT.C */

# include<stdio.h>
# include<malloc.h>

struct NODE
{
  int Info;
  struct NODE *Left_Child;
  struct NODE *Right_Child;
};

struct NODE *Binary_Tree (char *, int, int);
void Output(struct NODE *, int );

/* Function to insert an element into tree */

struct  NODE *  Binary_Tree (char *List, int Lower,
int Upper)
{
  struct NODE *Node;
  int Mid = (Lower + Upper)/2;
```

(Contd.)

```
 Node = (struct NODE *) malloc(sizeof(struct
 NODE));
 Node->Info = List [Mid];
 if ( Lower>= Upper)
 {
   Node->Left_Child = NULL;
   Node->Right_Child = NULL;
   return (Node);
 }

 if (Lower <= Mid - 1)
   Node->Left_Child = Binary_Tree (List, Lower, Mid
   - 1);
 else
   Node->Left_Child = NULL;
 if (Mid + 1 <= Upper)
   Node->Right_Child = Binary_Tree (List, Mid + 1,
   Upper);
 else
   Node->Right_Child = NULL;
 return(Node);
}

/* Output function */

void Output(struct NODE *T, int Level)
{
  int i;
  if (T)
  {
    Output(T->Right_Child, Level+1);
    printf("\n");
    for (i = 0; i < Level; i++)
      printf("   ");
    printf("%c", T->Info);
    Output(T->Left_Child, Level+1);
  }
}

/* Function main */

void main()
```

(Contd.)

```
{
  char List[100];
  int Number = 0;
  char Info ;
  char choice;
  struct NODE *T = (struct NODE *)
  malloc(sizeof(struct NODE));
  T = NULL;
  printf("\n Input choice 'b' to break:");
  choice = getchar();
  while(choice != 'b')
  {
    printf("\n Input information of the node: ");
    scanf("%c", &Info);
    List[Number++] = Info;
    fflush(stdin);
    printf("\n Input choice 'b' to break:");
    choice = getchar();
  }
  Number --;
  printf("\n Number of elements in the lsit is %d",
  Number);
  T = Binary_Tree(List, 0, Number);
  Output(T,1);
}
```

Program 4.

```
/* Create TREE */
/* CREAT_T.C */

# include<stdio.h>
# include<malloc.h>
struct NODE
{
  int Info;
  struct NODE *Left_Child;
  struct NODE *Right_Child;
};

struct NODE *Create_Tree (int , struct NODE *);
void Output(struct NODE *, int );
```

(Contd.)

```
/* Function to create a tree */

struct NODE * Create_Tree (int Info, struct NODE
*Node)
{
  if (Node == NULL)
  {
    Node = (struct NODE *) malloc( sizeof(struct
    NODE ));
    Node->Info = Info;
    Node->Left_Child = NULL;
    Node->Right_Child = NULL;
    return (Node);
  }

  /* Test for the left child */
  if (Node->Info >= Info )
    Node->Left_Child = Create_Tree (Info, Node-
    >Left_Child);
  else

/* Set all the rest of the elements as right child */

    Node->Right_Child = Create_Tree (Info, Node-
    >Right_Child);
  return(Node);
}

/* Output function */

void Output(struct NODE *T, int Level)
{
  int i;
  if (T)
  {
    Output(T->Right_Child, Level+1);
    printf("\n ");
    for (i = 0; i < Level; i++)
      printf("   ");
    printf("%d", T->Info);
```

(Contd.)

```
    printf("\n");
    Output(T->Left_Child, Level+1);
  }
}

/* Function main */

void main()
{
  int Info ;
  char choice;
  struct NODE *T = (struct NODE *)
  malloc(sizeof(struct NODE *));
  T = NULL;
  printf("\n Input choice 'b' to break:");
  choice = getchar();
  while(choice != 'b')
  {
    printf("\n Input information of the node: ");
    scanf("%d", &Info);
    T = Create_Tree (Info, T);
    printf("\n Tree is ");
    Output(T, 1);
    printf("\n Input choice 'b' to break:");
    choice = getchar();
  }
}
```

Program 5.

```
/* Deleting in Binary Tree */
/* DELET_BT.C */
# include<stdio.h>
# include<malloc.h>

struct NODE
{
  int Info;
  struct NODE *Left_Child;
  struct NODE *Right_Child;
};
```

(Contd.)

```
int depth;
void Output (struct NODE *, int );
struct NODE *Delet_Node (struct NODE *, int );
struct NODE *Create_Tree (int , struct NODE *);
struct NODE * DELE(struct NODE *, struct NODE *);

/* Output function */

void Output(struct NODE *T, int Level)
{
  int i;
  if (T)
  {
    Output(T->Right_Child, Level+1);
    printf("\n");
    for (i = 0; i < Level; i++)
      printf("  ");
    printf("%c", T->Info);
    Output(T->Left_Child, Level+1);
  }
}

/* Delete a node in the binary tree */

struct NODE * DELE(struct NODE *Node1, struct NODE
*Node)
{
  struct NODE *DNode;
  if (Node1->Right_Child != NULL)
    Node1->Right_Child = DELE(Node1->Right_Child,
    Node);
  else
  {
    DNode = Node1;
    Node->Info = Node1->Info;
    Node1 = Node1->Left_Child;
    free(DNode);
  }
  return (Node1);
}

/* Deletion in binary tree */
```

(Contd.)

```
struct NODE * Delet_Node (struct NODE *Node, int
Info)
{
  struct NODE *Temp;

  if (Node == NULL)
  {
    printf("\n Information does not exist in the
    above tree");
    return (Node);
  }
  else
  {
    if (Info < Node->Info )
      Node->Left_Child = Delet_Node (Node-
      >Left_Child, Info);
    else
      if (Info > Node->Info )

        Node->Left_Child = Delet_Node (Node-
        >Right_Child, Info);
      else
      {
        Temp = Node;
        if (Temp->Right_Child == NULL)
        {
          Node = Temp->Left_Child;
          free(Temp);
        }
        else
          if (Temp->Left_Child == NULL)
          {
            Node = Temp->Right_Child;
            free(Temp);
          }
          else
            Temp->Left_Child = DELE(Temp->Left_Child,
            Temp);
      }
  }
  return(Node);
}
```

(Contd.)

```
/* Create binary tree */

struct NODE *  Create_Tree (int Info, struct NODE
*Node)
{
  if (Node == NULL)
  {
    Node = (struct NODE *) malloc(sizeof(struct
    NODE));
    Node->Info = Info;
    Node->Left_Child = NULL;
    Node->Right_Child = NULL;
    return (Node);
  }

  /* Test for the left child */

  if (Info < Node->Info)

    Node->Left_Child = Create_Tree (Info, Node-
>Left_Child);
  else

    /* Test for the right child */

    if (Info >= Node->Info)
      Node->Right_Child = Create_Tree (Info, Node-
>Right_Child);
  return(Node);
}

/* Function main */

void main()
{
  int Number = 0;
  int Info ;
  char choice;
  int depth;
  struct NODE *T = (struct NODE *)
  malloc(sizeof(struct NODE));
  T = NULL;
  printf("\n Input choice 'b' to break:");
```

(Contd.)

```
choice = getchar();

while(choice != 'b')
{
  fflush(stdin);
  printf("\n Input information of the node: ");
  scanf("%c", &Info);
  T = Create_Tree(Info, T);
  Number++;
  fflush(stdin);
  printf("\n Input choice 'b' to break:");
  choice = getchar();
}
  fflush(stdin);
  printf("\n Number of elements in the list is
  %d", Number);
  printf("\n Tree is \n");
  Output(T, 1);
  printf("\n Input the information to which want
  remove from the above tree: ");
  scanf("%c", &Info);

T = Delet_Node(T, Info);
printf("\n Tree after deletion of a node: ");
Output(T, 1);
}
```

Program 6.

```
/*  Finding Depth of Binary Tree */
/* DEPTH_BT.C */

# include<stdio.h>
# include<malloc.h>

struct NODE
{
  char Info;
  struct NODE *Left_Child;
  struct NODE *Right_Child;
};
```

(Contd.)

```
int depth = 0;

void Output (struct NODE *, int );
int Depth (struct NODE *, int );
struct NODE *Create_Tree (char , struct NODE *);

/* Output function */

void Output(struct NODE *T, int Level)
{
  int i;
  if (T)
  {
    Output(T->Right_Child, Level+1);
    printf("\n");
    for (i = 0; i < Level; i++)
      printf("  ");
    printf("%c", T->Info);
    Output(T->Left_Child, Level+1);
  }
}

/* Find depth of the tree */

int Depth (struct NODE *Node, int Level)
{
  if (Node != NULL)
  {
    if (Level > depth)
      depth = Level;
    Depth (Node->Left_Child, Level + 1);
    Depth (Node->Right_Child, Level + 1);
  }
  return (depth);
}

/*  Create binary tree */
struct NODE *  Create_Tree (char Info, struct NODE
*Node)
{

  if (Node == NULL)
```

(Contd.)

```
  {
   Node = (struct NODE *) malloc(sizeof(struct
   NODE));
   Node->Info = Info;
   Node->Left_Child = NULL;
   Node->Right_Child = NULL;
   return (Node);
  }

  /* Test for the left child */

  if (Info < Node->Info)

   Node->Left_Child = Create_Tree (Info, Node-
>Left_Child);

  else

   /*  Test for the right child */

   if (Info > Node->Info)

     Node->Right_Child = Create_Tree (Info, Node-
     >Right_Child);
 return(Node);
}

/* Function main */

void main()
{
 int Number = 0;
 char Info ;
 char choice;
 int depth;
 struct NODE *T = (struct NODE *)
 malloc(sizeof(struct NODE));
 T = NULL;
 printf("\n Input choice 'b' to break:");
 choice = getchar();

 while(choice != 'b')
```

(Contd.)

```
  {
    fflush(stdin);
    printf("\n Input information of the node: ");
    scanf("%c", &Info);
    T = Create_Tree(Info, T);
    Number++;
    fflush(stdin);
    printf("\n Input choice 'b' to break:");
    choice = getchar();
  }
    printf("\n Number of elements in the list is
    %d", Number);
    printf("\n Tree is \n");
    Output(T, 1);

    depth = Depth(T, 0);
    printf("\n Depth of the above tree is:  %d",
    depth);
}
```

Program 7.

```
/* Insertion in a Binary Tree */
/* INSERT.C */

# include<stdio.h>

struct NODE
{
  char Info;
  struct NODE *Left_Child;
  struct NODE *Right_Child;
};

int flag = 0;
struct NODE *Binary_Tree (char *, int, int);
void Output(struct NODE *, int );
struct NODE *Insert_Node(struct NODE *, char);

/* Function to create an binary tree */

struct NODE *  Binary_Tree (char *List, int Lower,
```

(Contd.)

```
int Upper)
{
  struct NODE *Node;
  int Mid = (Lower + Upper)/2;
  Node = (struct NODE*) malloc(sizeof(struct
  NODE));

  Node->Info = List [Mid];
  if ( Lower>= Upper)
  {
    Node->Left_Child = NULL;
    Node->Right_Child = NULL;
    return (Node);
  }

  if (Lower <= Mid - 1)
    Node->Left_Child = Binary_Tree (List, Lower, Mid
    - 1);
  else
    Node->Left_Child = NULL;
  if (Mid + 1 <= Upper)
    Node->Right_Child = Binary_Tree (List, Mid + 1,
    Upper);
  else
    Node->Right_Child = NULL;
    return(Node);
}

/* Output function */

void Output(struct NODE *T, int Level)
{
  int i;
  if (T)
  {
    Output(T->Right_Child, Level+1);
    printf("\n");
    for (i = 0; i < Level; i++)
      printf("   ");
    printf("%c", T->Info);
    Output(T->Left_Child, Level+1);
  }
```

(Contd.)

```
}

/* Insert a node in the tree */

struct NODE * Insert_Node(struct NODE *Node, char
Info)
{
  if (Node == NULL)
  {
    Node = (struct NODE *) malloc(sizeof(struct
    NODE));
    Node->Info = Info;
    Node->Left_Child = NULL;
    Node->Right_Child = NULL;
    return (Node);
  }

  /* Test for the left child   */

  if (Node->Info >= Info )
    Node->Left_Child = Insert_Node (Node-
    >Left_Child, Info);
  else

    /* Set all the rest of the elements as right
child */
    Node->Right_Child = Insert_Node (Node-
>Right_Child, Info);
  return(Node);
}

/* Function main */

void main()
{
  char List[100];
  int Number = 0;
  char Info ;
  char choice;
  struct NODE *T = (struct NODE*) malloc
  (sizeof(struct NODE));
  T = NULL;
```

(Contd.)

```
    printf("\n Input choice 'b' to break:");
    choice = getchar();
    while(choice != 'b')
    {
      fflush(stdin);
      printf("\n Input information of the node: ");
      scanf("%c", &Info);
      List[Number++] = Info;
      fflush(stdin);
      printf("\n Input choice 'b' to break:");
      choice = getchar();
    }
    Number --;
    printf("\n Number of elements in the list is %d",
    Number+1);
    T = Binary_Tree(List, 0, Number);
    printf("\n Tree is \n");
    Output(T,1);
    fflush(stdin);
    printf("\n Input the information of the node to
    which want to insert: ");
    scanf("%c", &Info);
    T = Insert_Node(T, Info);
    printf("\n Tree is \n");
    Output(T, 1);
}
```

Program 8.

```
/* Searching Binary Tree */
/* SEARCH_B.C */

# include<stdio.h>
# include<malloc.h>

struct NODE
{
  char Info;
  struct NODE *Left_Child;
  struct NODE *Right_Child;
};
```

(Contd.)

```
int flag = 0;
struct NODE *Binary_Tree (char *, int, int);
void Output(struct NODE *, int );
int Search_Node(struct NODE *, char);

/* Function to create an binary tree */

struct NODE *  Binary_Tree (char *List, int Lower,
int Upper)
{
 struct NODE *Node;
 int Mid = (Lower + Upper)/2;
 Node = (struct NODE*) malloc(sizeof(struct
 NODE));

 Node->Info = List [Mid];
 if ( Lower>= Upper)
 {
  Node->Left_Child = NULL;
  Node->Right_Child = NULL;
  return (Node);
 }
 if (Lower <= Mid - 1)
  Node->Left_Child = Binary_Tree (List, Lower, Mid
  - 1);
 else
  Node->Left_Child = NULL;
 if (Mid + 1 <= Upper)
  Node->Right_Child = Binary_Tree (List, Mid + 1,
  Upper);
 else
  Node->Right_Child = NULL;
 return(Node);
}

/* Output function */

void Output(struct NODE *T, int Level)
{
 int i;
 if (T)
 {
```

(Contd.)

```
      Output(T->Right_Child, Level+1);
      printf("\n");
      for (i = 0; i < Level; i++)
        printf("   ");
      printf("%c", T->Info);
      Output(T->Left_Child, Level+1);
    }
}

/* Insert a node in the tree */

int Search_Node(struct NODE *Node, char Info)
{
  while (Node != NULL)
  {
    if (Node->Info == Info)
    {
      flag = 1;
      return(flag);
    }
    else
      if(Info < Node->Info)
      {
        Node = Node->Left_Child;
      }
      else
      {
        Node = Node->Right_Child;
      }
  }
  return(flag);
}

/* Function main */

void main()
{
  int flag;
  char List[100];
  int Number = 0;
  char Info ;
  char choice;
```

(Contd.)

```
struct NODE *T = (struct NODE *)
malloc(sizeof(struct NODE));
T = NULL;
printf("\n Input choice 'b' to break:");
choice = getchar();
while(choice != 'b')
{
  fflush(stdin);
  printf("\n Input information of the node: ");
  scanf("%c", &Info);
  List[Number++] = Info;
  fflush(stdin);
  printf("\n Input choice 'b' to break:");
  choice = getchar();
}
Number --;
printf("\n Number of elements in the list is %d",
Number+1);
T = Binary_Tree(List, 0, Number);
printf("\n Tree is \n");
Output(T, 1);
fflush(stdin);
printf("\n Input the information of the node to
which want to search: ");
scanf("%c", &Info);
flag = Search_Node(T, Info);
if (flag)
{
  printf("\n Search is successful \n");
}
else
  printf("Search unsuccessful");
}
```

Graph

Program 1.

```
/* BREADTH FIRST SEARCH TECHNIQUE */
/* BFS.C */

# include<stdio.h>
# define size 20
# define T 1
# define F 0

struct Edge
{
  int terminal;
  struct Edge *next;
};

struct Vertex
{
  int visit;
  int vertex_no;
  char info;
  int path_length;
  struct Edge *Edge_Ptr;
};
struct Q
{
  int info;
  struct Q *next;
};

void Table(int , int matrix [size][size], struct
Vertex vert[size]);
struct Edge *Insert_Vertex (int , struct Edge *);
```

(Contd.)

```
void BFS ( int , struct Vertex vert [size]);
void Input(int, int mat [size][size]);
void Output(int number, int mat [size][size]);
struct Q *Insert_Queue(int vertex_no, struct Q
*first);
struct Q *Delete_Queue(int *vertex_no, struct Q
*first);

/* Insert vertex into connectivity list */

struct Edge * Insert_Vertex (int vertex_no, struct
Edge
*first)          {
  struct Edge *new1, *current;
  new1 = (struct Edge *) malloc(sizeof(struct
  Edge));
  new1->terminal = vertex_no;
  new1->next = NULL;
  if (!first)
    return (new1);
  for (current = first; current->next; current =
  current->next);
  current->next = new1;
  return (first);
}

/* Insert vertices into queue */

struct Q * Insert_Queue(int vertex_no, struct Q
*first)
{
  struct Q *new1, *current;
  new1 =(struct Q *) malloc(sizeof(struct Q));
  new1->info = vertex_no;
  new1->next = NULL;
  if (!first)
    return (new1);
  for (current = first; current->next; current =
  current->next);
  current->next = new1;
  return (first);
}
struct  Q * Delete_Queue(int *vertex_no, struct Q
```

(Contd.)

```
*first)
{
  struct Q *previous;
  if (!first)
    return (NULL);
  *vertex_no = first->info;
  previous = first;
  first = first->next;
  free(previous);
  return (first);
}

/* Initializing entries */

void Table(int vertex_num, int matrix [size][size],
struct   Vertex vert[size])
{
  int i, j;
  for (i = 0; i < vertex_num; i++)
  {
    vert [i].visit = F;
    vert [i].vertex_no = i+1;
    vert [i].info = 'A'+ i;
    vert [i].path_length = 0;
    vert [i].Edge_Ptr = NULL;
  }

  for (i =0; i < vertex_num ; i++)
    for (j =0; j < vertex_num ; j++)
      if (matrix [i][j] > 0 )
        vert [i].Edge_Ptr = Insert_Vertex (j, vert
        [i].Edge_Ptr);
}

/* Computing path length */

void BFS ( int index, struct Vertex vert [size])
{
  struct Q  *queue = NULL;
  struct Edge *Link;
  vert [index].visit = T;
  queue = Insert_Queue(index, queue);
```

(Contd.)

```
  while(queue)
  {
    queue = Delete_Queue(&index, queue);
    for ( Link = vert [index].Edge_Ptr; Link; Link =
    Link->next)
    {
      if (vert [Link->terminal].visit == F)
      {
        vert[Link->terminal].visit = T;
        vert[Link->
        terminal].path_length=vert[index].
        path_length+1;
        queue = Insert_Queue(Link->terminal, queue);
      }
    }
  }
}

/* Input function to read adjacency matrix */

void Input(int number, int mat [size][size])
{
  int i, j;
  printf("\n Input the adjacency matrix \n");
  for (i =0; i < number; i++)
  {
    for (j=0; j < number; j ++)
    {
      scanf("%d", &mat [i][j]);
    }
    printf("\n");
  }
}

/* Output function to display adjacency matrix */

void Output(int number, int mat [size][size])
{
  int i, j;
  printf("\n Adjacency matrix \n");
  for (i =0; i < number; i++)
  {
```

(Contd.)

```
      for (j=0; j < number; j ++)
      {
        printf("   %d", mat [i][j]);
      }
      printf("\n");
    }
  }

  /* Function main */
  void  main()
  {
    int i, number, index;
    int mat [size][size];
    struct Vertex vert [size];
    struct Edge *List;
    printf("\n Input the number of vertices in the
    graph: ");
    scanf("%d", &number);
    Input(number, mat);
    Output(number, mat);
    Table(number, mat, vert);
    printf("\n Input the starting vertex 0- %d
    :",number-1);
    scanf("%d", &index);
    BFS (index, vert);
    printf("\n Path length of the vertex from %c",
    vert[index].info);
    printf("\n Vertex Length Vertex Connectivity \n
    ");
    for (i = 0; i < number; i++)
    {
      printf("\n   %c    %d   ",vert[i].info,
      vert[i].path_length);
      for (List= vert[i].Edge_Ptr; List; List = List-
      >next)
      {
        printf(" ");
        putchar(List->terminal+'A');
      }
    }
  }
```

Program 2.

```
/* DEPTH FIRST SEARCH TECHNIQUE */
/* DFS.C */

# include<stdio.h>
# define size 20
# define T 1
# define F 0

struct Edge
{
  int terminal;
  struct Edge *next;
};
struct Vertex
{
  int visit;
  int vertex_no;
  char info;
  int path_length;
  struct Edge *Edge_Ptr;
};
  void Table(int , int matrix [size][size], struct
  Vertex vert[size]);
  struct Edge *Insert_Vertex (int , struct Edge *);
  void DFS ( int , int *dist, struct Vertex vert
  [size]);
  void Input(int, int a [size][size]);
  void Output(int, int a [size][size]);

struct Edge * Insert_Vertex (int vertex_no, struct
Edge *first)
{
  struct Edge *new1, *current;
  new1 = (struct Edge *) malloc(sizeof(struct
  Edge));
  new1->terminal = vertex_no;
  new1->next = NULL;
  if (!first)
    return (new1);
  for (current = first; current->next; current =
```

(Contd.)

```
current->next);
  current->next = new1;
  return (first);
}

/* Initializing entries */

void Table(int vertex_num, int matrix [size][size],
struct Vertex vert[size])
{
  int i, j;
  for (i = 0; i < vertex_num; i++)
  {
    vert [i].visit = F;
    vert [i].vertex_no = i+1;
    vert [i].info = 'A'+ i;
    vert [i].path_length = 0;
    vert [i].Edge_Ptr = NULL;
  }

  for (i =0; i < vertex_num ; i++)
    for (j =0; j < vertex_num ; j++)
      if (matrix [i][j] > 0)
        vert [i].Edge_Ptr = Insert_Vertex (j, vert
        [i].Edge_Ptr);
}

/* Computing path length */
void DFS ( int index, int *dist,
struct Vertex vert [size])
{
  struct Edge *Link;
  vert [index].visit = T;
  vert [index].path_length = *dist;
  *dist += 1;
  for ( Link = vert [index].Edge_Ptr; Link; Link =
  Link->next)
    if (vert [Link->terminal].visit == F)
      DFS (Link->terminal, dist, vert);
}

/* Input function to read adjacency matrix */
```

(Contd.)

```
void Input(int number, int a [size][size])
{
  int i, j;
  printf("\n Input the adjacency matrix \n");

  for (i =0; i < number; i++)
  {
   for (j=0; j < number; j ++)
   {
     scanf("%d", &a [i][j]);
   }
   printf("\n");
  }
}

/* Output function */
void Output(int number, int a [size][size])
{
  int i, j;
  printf("\n Adjacency matrix \n");
  for (i = 0; i < number; i++)
  {
   for (j = 0; j < number; j ++)
   {
     printf("   %d", a [i][j]);
   }
   printf("\n");
  }
}

/* Function main */
void  main()
{
  int i;
  int number, index, dist;
  int a [size][size];
  struct Vertex vert [size];
  struct Edge *List;
  printf("\n Input the number of vertices in the
  graph: ");
  scanf("%d", &number);
  Input(number, a);
```

(Contd.)

```
    Output(number, a);

    Table(number, a, vert);
    printf("\n Input the starting vertex 0- %d:",
    number-1);
    scanf("%d", &index);
    dist = 0;
    DFS (index, &dist, vert);
    printf("\n Path length of the vertex from %c",
    vert[index].info);
    printf("\n Vertex Length Vertex Connectivity \n
    ");
    for (i = 0; i < number; i++)
    {
      printf("\n  %c  %d   ", vert[i].info,
      vert[i].path_length);
      for (List= vert[i].Edge_Ptr; List; List = List-
      >next)
      {
        printf(" ");
        putchar(List->terminal+'A');
      }
    }
}
```

Program 3.

```
/* DIJKSTRA METHOD */
/* DIJKSTRA.C*/

# include<stdio.h>

# define size 20
# define P 1
# define T 0
# define infinity 9999

struct Label
{
  int predecessor;
  int length;
  int flag;
```

(Contd.)

```
};

int k, min, count;
struct Label state[size];
int visit_path[size];

int Short_Path(int a[size][size], int , int , int,
int path [size], int *);
void Input(int , int a[size][size]);
void Output(int , int a[size][size]);

/* Shortest path computing function */
int  Short_Path(int a[size][size], int n, int s,
int t,
int path[size], int *dist)
{
  int i;
  int t1, t2;
  *dist = 0;

  for(i = 1; i <= n; i ++)
  {
    state[i].predecessor = 0;
    state[i].length = infinity ;
    state[i].flag = T;
  }
  /* Make source vertex permanent */
  state[s].predecessor = 0;
  state[s].length = 0;
  state[s].flag = P;

  /* Start from source vertex */

  k = s;
  do
  {
 /* Check all the paths from kth vertex and find
 their distance from k vertex */
    for ( i = 1; i <= n; i++)
    {
      if ((a[k][i] > 0) && (state[i].flag == T))
      {
```

(Contd.)

```
            if ((state[k].length + a[k][i]) <
            state[i].length)
            {
              state[i].predecessor = k;
              state[i].length = state[k].length +
              a[k][i];
            }
          }
        }
        min = infinity;
        k = 0;
        for ( i =1; i <= n; i++)
        {
          if ((state[i].flag == T) && (state[i].length <
          min))
          {
            min = state[i].length;
            k = i;
          }
        }
        if ( k==0)
          return (0);
        state[k].flag = P;
      } while(k != t);

      /* Store optimal path */
      k = t;
      count = 1;
      do
      {

        visit_path[count] = k;
        count ++;
        k = state[k].predecessor;
      } while(k!= 0);

    /* Reverse the vertices since algorithm stores path
    in reverse direction */

      count --;
      for ( i = 1; i <= count ; i++)
        path[i] = visit_path[count-i+1];
```

(Contd.)

```
  for ( i = 1; i < count ; i ++)
  {
    t1 = path[i];
    t2 = path [i+1];
    *dist += a[t1][t2];
  }
  return (count);
}

/* Input function */
void Input(int n, int a[size][size])
{
  int i, j;
  printf("\n Input adjacency matrix \n");
  for(i =0; i < n; i++)
  {
    for(j =0; j < n; j++)
    {
      scanf("%d", &a[i][j]);
    }
    printf("\n");
  }
}

/* Output function */
void Output(int n, int a[size][size])
{
  int i, j;
  printf("\n Adjacency matrix \n");
  for(i =0; i < n; i++)
  {
    for(j =0; j < n; j++)
    {
      printf("  %d", a[i][j]);
    }
    printf("\n");
  }
}

/* Function main */

void main()
```

(Contd.)

```
{
  int a[size][size];
  int path [size];
  int org, dest, dist;
  int count, i, n;

  printf("\n Input the number of vertices in the
  graph: ");
  scanf("%d", &n);

  Input(n,a);
  Output(n,a);

  printf("\n Input strating vertex: ");
  scanf("%d", &org);
  printf("\n Input destination: ");
  scanf("%d", &dest);
  count = Short_Path(a, n, org, dest, path, &dist);
  if (dist)
  {
    printf("\n Shortest path: %d", path[1]);
    for (i = 2; i<=count; i++);
    printf(" => %d", path[i]);
    printf("\n Minimum distance = %i", dist);
  }
  else
    printf("\n Path does not exist \n");
}
```

Program 4.

```
/* FLYOD'S METHOD */
/* FLYOD.C */

 # include<stdio.h>

 # define Infinity 9999
 # define size 20

  int i,k,j;
  void Input(int , int a[size][size]);
   void Output(int , int a[size][size]);
```

(Contd.)

```
void Flyod(int , int a[size][size], int
r[size][size]);

/* Input function */

void Input(int n, int a[size][size])
  {
    int i, j;
    printf("\n Input adjacency matrix\n");
    for (i = 0; i < n; i++)
{
  for (j = 0; j < n; j++)
  {
    scanf("%d", &a[i][j]);
  }
    printf("\n");
  }
 }

/* Output function */

void Output (int n, int a[size][size])
   {
   int i, j;
   for (i =0; i < n; i++)
{
  for (j =0; j < n; j++)
  {
    printf(" %d", a[i][j]);
  }
 printf("\n");
    }
  }

/* Shortest path evaluation function */

void Flyod(int n, int a[size][size], int
r[size][size])
    {
 for (i = 0; i < n; i ++)
   a[i][i] = 0; /* Set diagonal elements zero */
   printf("\n After setting diagonal elements to
```

(Contd.)

```
zero \n");
     Output(n, a);
     for (i = 0; i < n; i++)
        {
         for (j = 0; j < n; j++)
          {
    if ((a[i][j] == 0) && (i != j))
     r[i][j] = Infinity;
     else
      r[i][j] = a[i][j];
          }
       }
       printf("\n Replacing zeros by very large
       value \n");
       Output(n, r);
    for (k = 0; k < n; k++)
    {
     for (i = 0; i < n; i++)
       {
        for (j = 0; j < n; j++)
         {
             if (r[i][k] + r[k][j]< r[i][j])
         {
             printf("\n r[%d][%d] = %d ", i, k,
             r[i][k]);
             printf("\n r[%d][%d] = %d ", k, j,
             r[k][j]);
             printf("\n r[%d][%d] = %d ", i, j,
             r[i][j]);
             r[i][j] = r[i][k] +  r[k][j];
             printf("\n r[%d][%d] = r[%d][%d] +
             r[%d][%d] = %d ", i, j, i, k, k, j,
             r[i][j]);
         }
        else
         {
             r[i][j] = r[i][j];
             printf("\n r[%d][%d] = r[%d][%d] = %d
             ", i, j, i, j, r[i][j]);
         }
        }
       printf("\n");
```

(Contd.)

```
    }
    printf("\n Step %d \n", k);
    Output (n,r);
  }
    }

/* Function main */

   void main()
      {
   int a[size][size];
   int r[size][size];
   int n;
   printf("\n Input number of vertices in the
   graph: ");
   scanf("%d", &n);
   Input(n,a);
   printf("\n Adjacency matrix\n");
   Output(n,a);
   Flyod(n,a,r);
   printf("\n Shortest path matrix \n");
   Output(n,r);
}
```

Program 5.

```
/* SHORTEST PATH */
/* SPATH.C */

 # include<stdio.h>
 # define size 10
 # define infinity 9999

   int a[size][size];
   int m[size][size];
   int i,k,j;
   int n;

   void Input ();
   void Short ();
   void Output ();
```

(Contd.)

```
/* Input function */

void Input()
    {
      printf("\n Input the number of vetices: ");
      scanf("%d", &n);
      printf("\n Input adjacency matrix\n");
      for (i = 0; i < n; i++)
      {
        for (j = 0; j < n; j++)
        {
          scanf("%d", &a[i][j]);
        }
        printf("\n");
      }
        printf("\n Adjacency matrix \n");
        for ( i = 0; i < n; i++)
        {
          for ( j = 0; j < n; j++)
          {
            printf("  %i", a[i][j]);
          }
        printf("\n");
      }
    }

/* Output function */

void Output()
    {
      for ( i = 0; i < n; i++)
        {
          for ( j = 0; j < n; j++)
            {
              printf("   %d", m[i][j]);
            }
          printf("\n");
        }
    }

/* Shortest path function */
```

(Contd.)

```
void  Short ()

    /* Initialization of matrix m */

       for ( i = 0; i < n; i++)
         {
           for ( j = 0; j < n; j++)
           {
               if (a[i][j] == 0)
               m[i][j] = infinity;
               else
               m[i][j] = a[i][j];
           }
       }
printf("\n Adjacency matrix after replacing zeros
by very large value"); Output();

/*  Shortest path evaluation start from here */

      for ( k = 0; k < n; k++)
         {
              for ( i = 0; i < n; i++)
                {
                  for ( j = 0; j < n; j++)
                    {
                      if ( m [i][j] <= m [i][k] + m
                      [k][j] )
                      m [i][j] = m [i][j];
                    . else
              m [i][j] = m[i][k] + m [k][j];
         }
   }
   printf("\n STEP %d \n", k);
   Output();
       }
    }

/* Function main */

  void main()
       {
  Input();
```

(Contd.)

```
    Short();
    printf("\n Shortest path matrix is as
    follows\n");
    Output();
}
```

Program 6.

```
/* SHORTEST PATH */
/* WARSHALL.C */

# include<stdio.h>
# define size 10

int a [size][size];
int p [size][size];
int i,k,j;
int n;

void Input ();
void Warshall ();
void Output ();

/* Input function */

void Input()
{
  printf("\n Input the number of vertices: ");
  scanf("%d", &n);
  printf("\n Input adjency matrix\n");
  for ( i = 0; i < n; i++)
  {
    for ( j = 0; j < n; j++)
    {
      scanf("%d", &a[i][j]);
    }
    printf("\n");
  }
  printf("\n Adjency matrix \n");
  for ( i = 0; i < n; i++)
  {
    for ( j = 0; j < n; j++)
```

(Contd.)

```
    {
    printf(" %d", a[i][j]);
    }
    printf("\n");
  }
}

/* Output function */

void  Output()
{
  for ( i = 0; i < n; i++)
  {
    for ( j = 0; j < n; j++)
    {
    printf("  %d", p [i][j]);
    }
    printf("\n");
  }
}

/* Shortest path function */

void Warshall ()
{
  /* Initialization of matrix m */

  for ( i = 0; i < n; i++)
  {
    for ( j = 0; j < n; j++)
    {
      if (a[i][j] == 0)
        p [i][j] = 0;
      else
        p[i][j] = 1;
    }
  }

  /* Shortest Path evaluation start from here */

  for ( k = 0; k < n; k++)
  {
```

(Contd.)

```
    for ( i = 0; i < n; i++)
    {
      for ( j = 0; j < n; j++)
      {
        p[i][j] = p[i][j] | ( p[i][k] & p[k][j]);
      }
    }
  }
}
/* Function main */

void main()
{
  Input ();
  Warshall ();
  printf("\n Path matrix:\n");
  Output ();
}
```